CHRISTMAS
2012

To GRANDPA

From GRANDMA

WHAT BRITAIN HAS DONE

1939–1945

WHAT BRITAIN HAS DONE

1939–1945

A Selection of Outstanding Facts and Figures

Introduction by
Richard Overy

Issued by the
Ministry of Information

Atlantic Books
LONDON

This book was first published by the Ministry of Information in 1945.

Introduction first published in Great Britain in 2007 by Atlantic Books, an imprint of Grove Atlantic Ltd.

9 8 7 6 5 4 3 2 1

A CIP catalogue record for this book is available from the British Library.

ISBN 978 1 84354 680 1

All maps by Jeff Edwards
Text design by Lindsay Nash

Printed in Malta

Atlantic Books
An imprint of Grove Atlantic Ltd
Ormond House
26–27 Boswell Street
London WC1N 3JZ

CONTENTS

MAPS

INTRODUCTION

What did Britain do during the Second World War? There is certainly no simple answer to this question, and no answer on which everyone might agree. If a cross-section of the public were stopped in the street and asked what Britain did in the war the most likely answer would be: 'Britain defeated Hitler.' This is an incomplete but not a wrong answer. For most Britons who found themselves at war on 3 September 1939 the contest boiled down to ridding the world of Hitler. He became the lightning conductor for all the fears and hatreds of a Western world obsessively anxious that fascism spelt the end of civilization. Emerging into the grey dawn of victory in May 1945, knowing that Hitler was dead by his own hand and Germany surrendered, the British people could be forgiven for thinking that they had done the job they started out on six years before.

It was evident in 1945, however, that a great deal had changed in the six years of war. Britain declared war in 1939 alongside France. By June 1940 her ally was defeated and occupied by the German enemy. There was no serious prospect of defeating Germany, and from June 1940 Italy too, without powerful allies. They came unexpectedly in the shape of the Soviet Union, following Axis invasion in June

1941, and the United States as a result of the Japanese attack on Pearl Harbor on 7 December that same year. The three states fought as a Grand Alliance – though there was no formal alliance between them – and at the end of the war their massive military and economic strength led to the defeat first of Italy, in 1943, then Germany and Japan in 1945. By that date the Soviet Union and the United States had been transformed into the superpowers of the post-war world, their sheer size and fighting power dwarfing their British ally. When the so-called 'Big Three' met in the Crimean city of Yalta in February 1945 to decide the political shape of Europe after the war, the British Prime Minister, Winston Churchill, confessed that he felt ill at ease with his companions. Britain had begun the war as one of the world's greatest powers; she finished it reduced in stature by the giant powers she fought with.

This may well explain why the Ministry of Information a few months later issued the booklet *What Britain Has Done*. Diminished in scale by the shifting balance of power, it must have seemed all the more necessary to blow Britain's own trumpet as loudly as possible at the end of the European war. The long catalogue of Britain's military, economic and social achievements was designed to appeal not just to a British public denied hard facts and figures for a long time, but to an international community increasingly dazzled by or fearful of the new superpowers. It is more than a mere rendering of accounts: here is the British government staking its claim for a share of the limelight of unconditional victory.

In the years since the Second World War that claim has scarcely dimmed with the British public, but it has been severely scrutinized by later historians of the conflict who focus more than ever on the vast and lethal Eastern Front, where the back of the German armed forces was broken, or the multi-front war waged by the United States, whose massive productive power fuelled her allies and nourished her own inexperienced armed forces. The costliest of Britain's campaigns, the mass bombing of German industrial cities, has been condemned by its critics as wasteful and strategically redundant. Britain's wartime role has been placed firmly in an unflattering historical perspective. The Suez crisis in 1956, when Britain was compelled by the United States and the Soviet Union to abandon an attack on Egypt for nationalizing the Suez Canal, showed how swiftly Britain's international standing had declined.

In that sense *What Britain Has Done* is a timely reminder in today's world that the British war effort was prolonged, costly and far from negligible. The figures for war production, food production and the restriction of consumer goods show a high degree of national mobilization, though they fall short of the claim made here that Britain sacrificed living standards and mobilized for total war more extensively than any other combatant. This was a cherished self-perception which lives on more than sixty years later, but it is in many respects misleading. Both Germany and the Soviet Union imposed higher sacrifices and mobilised more ruthlessly. By 1945 half the native German workforce was female; more than four-fifths of the workers in Soviet agriculture were women. In the Soviet Union production for civilians was pared to the bone; in Germany, even as early as 1940, consumer living standards fell faster and further than they did in Britain.[1] None of this was known in Britain at the time, and what intelligence information existed persuaded the British authorities that they had indeed mobilized for total war more extensively than either ally or enemy.

Yet it is the military side of the conflict that takes the lion's share of what follows. It is easy to show that many of the claims made in May 1945 were exaggerated or partisan;

errors of strategy and military incompetence are not likely to feature in the celebration of a momentous victory, and they are absent entirely here. The picture presented is remarkable not only for what is missing but for what it does reveal about the shape of Britain's war effort. The war Britain fought was a truly global war because Britain was at the heart of a large world empire. Apart from the few months of air warfare in 1940 and 1941, Britain fought her war on other people's soil, or in international waters. In France, Italy, the Soviet Union, Germany, and throughout Eastern Europe the war was fought on or across the national territory of the combatant powers. Only Britain, and later the United States, was able to choose to fight where her own territory and people were not directly threatened by fighting, occupation and resistance. That this was possible was due to two things: the scale of British naval power and the extensive exploitation of imperial resources.

The most striking aspect of the military account is the disproportionate space devoted to the conduct of naval operations and the merchant fleet. In the original booklet this amounted to eleven and a half pages (if the blockade is added the total is almost fifteen); the army and the air forces were given six and a half pages each. In an age when Britain has at best an exiguous naval force it is easy to forget that in the 1940s Britain's national security and global reach were dependent to a very great extent on the Royal Navy. The role of the navy, including Britain's effective submarine arm (which seldom receives the historical attention it deserves) was manifold. Protecting convoys, blockading German-occupied Europe, keeping open the sea lanes in the Mediterranean and the major oceans, carrying troops and supplies, all of this was essential if Britain was to avoid a fight on her own territory. The naval threat played an important part in inhibiting Hitler's plans for Operation Sealion, the invasion of southern England in autumn 1940, which has usually been attributed to the efforts of Fighter Command in the Battle of Britain.[2] The navy made possible the invasion of Normandy in June 1944, when a colossal armada of 2,700 vessels was organized to carry out and support the combined operation – one of the most remarkable organizational achievements of the war. The navy fought a continuous and unstinting campaign against the German submarine in the Atlantic and the Italian navy in the Mediterranean, which made it possible to supply the British war effort and to ship the war effort of the United States in relative safety across 3,000 miles of water. Without a large and experienced navy Britain's war would have come to an end in 1940 or 1941, however determined the will to resist.

The global reach of Britain's naval power also underlines the imperial nature of Britain's war. This was a reality so important to Britain's war effort that its muted appearance in *What Britain Has Done* is immediately evident. The Empire is mentioned for the first time only on page 19 [page 6 of the original booklet], and it hardly features thereafter. The focus on Britain masks the extent to which this was a war fought by the British Empire and Commonwealth as a whole. Britain, despite Churchill's rhetoric of 1940, was never 'alone'. To readers born long after the demise of Britain's empire in the twenty years following the war it might be puzzling to find that Britain fought the war against Hitler in the grasslands and deserts of East and North Africa, the jungles of Madagascar and Burma and the oil-rich Middle East, before taking the war in 1943 into continental Europe. Of course, the war against Hitler turned by 1940 and 1941 into a war against the imperial ambitions of Italy and Japan as well, but these conflicts mattered only because they threatened the wide necklace of colonies, protectorates and Dominions that stretched around one-third of the globe. Indeed, for much of the war Britain fought a set of old-style imperial wars to protect her eastern Empire and her African colonies, and to defend nominally independent states such as Egypt and Iraq, which in fact hosted British forces whether they liked it or not.

The imperial nature of Britain's war effort also meant that the Empire contributed alongside the motherland. No account of what Britain did during the war is enough on its own because throughout the conflict Britain relied on men, money and supplies from around the world. Canada, for example, so often written out of narratives of Britain's war, mobilized a staggering 1.5 million in the armed forces out of a population of just 12 million. The Canadian government supplied $4 billion in loans and produced over 750,000 military vehicles.[3] In all the major campaigns by air and on land Empire divisions fought alongside British. Indeed, the curious insistence in *What Britain Has Done* on showing that a significant proportion of army divisions were 'British' side-steps the fact that the rest of the armies were from Canada, India, Australia, New Zealand and South Africa (to say nothing of those Empire recruits from colonial Africa and the Caribbean who worked on ships or served as military labour). None of this diminishes what Britain achieved, but it puts it into a necessary context. Churchill above all saw his role as an imperial leader, holding together an imperial coalition without which Britain 'alone' would have struggled to survive.

Nothing will strike the modern reader more oddly than the many claims made about the extraordinary battlefield achievements of the British (and Empire) armies. On page 8 [page 3 of the original booklet], the defeat of Italian armies in Ethiopia and the eventual defeat of a combined Italian-German force in North Africa are described immodestly as among 'the most extensive and the most successful in all history'. The arduous defeat of a disorganized Italian and colonial army in East Africa, and the long-drawn-out see-saw in the North African desert against Italian forces and a handful of German divisions were sideshows in comparison with the wars in the Soviet Union or the Sino–Japanese war. They mattered to Britain because they secured the Empire from further threat, but in the long annals of war they are unlikely to feature high up the list. Up to the autumn of 1942 the British army had suffered a series of humiliating defeats, none more inglorious than the defeat in Malaya and Singapore of a force very much larger than the invading Japanese army. The British Governor of Singapore was alleged to have told the British commander, General Arthur Percival, 'Well, I suppose you'll see the little men off,' when news of Japanese incursions arrived.[4] Instead more than 100,000 British and Empire troops entered captivity. In Norway, in France, in Greece and Crete, wherever the British army was tested it was rudely expelled. Victory at last at El Alamein in October 1942 came partly because of the shrewd skills of General Bernard Montgomery, who led Allied forces, but partly because by then the balance of tanks, air-craft, supplies and experienced troops greatly exceeded the number they faced. Opinion on the quality of British fighting power in the Normandy campaign remains divided.

Arguably, the one area where Britain's military effort made a difference was the bombing war against Germany, but this gets only a single page in the original booklet, under the heading of 'economic blockade'. This in itself is an inter-esting reflection of the view early in the war that bombing was complementary to the economic war being waged against Germany, whose whole shape was dictated by eco-nomic intelligence fed to Bomber Command by the Ministry of Economic Warfare. But it scarcely does credit to a campaign that absorbed a large proportion of Britain's war effort, involved the death of 55,000 airmen, and inhibited in a variety of ways Germany's capacity to make war. In the course of the city-bombing campaign over 420,000 German civilians were killed, a high proportion of them being women and children. There is no hint here of the randomness of British bombing attacks, which half a century later have provoked a powerful indictment of Britain's apparent indifference to the destruction of civilian lives and property.[5] Instead, the account of bombing reads rather like the end-of-year speech of a dull managing director to the company shareholders.

What Britain Has Done is full of facts and figures. The imponderables of war – the quality of leadership, the morale of the people, the advantages or disadvantages of one political system over another – feature hardly at all. Only at the very end is there consideration of the 'British spirit', a factor, it is claimed, greater than any strategic or industrial effort. It is impossible to measure, but the fact that it is ascribed characteristics such as 'dogged endeavour' and 'perseverance' suggests that staying power rather than passion was the quality of Britain's war. This was part of a self-image constructed early in the war, and it has survived in iconographic form as, among other things, 'the Dunkirk spirit'. No doubt the capacity of Britain's people to endure was solid enough. It was never severely tested except during the Blitz; Britain was not occupied nor was its countryside raked over by the fires of war. Yet on the day before *What Britain Has Done* was published the British population was convulsed with the passionate exuberance of victory. Whatever the statistical record of sacrifice, they were simply glad that the war against Hitler was over.

Richard Overy
Exeter, May 2007

Notes

1 See, for example, M. Harrison, *The Economics of World War II: Six Great Powers in International Comparison* (Cambridge, 1998) and R. J. Overy, *War and Economy in the Third Reich* (Oxford, 1994).

2 This view has recently been argued very forcefully in D. Robinson, *Invasion 1940: Did the Battle of Britain alone Stop Hitler?* (London, 2006).

3 A. Jackson, *The British Empire and the Second World War* (London, 2006), pp. 59–63.

4 A. Warren, *Singapore 1942: Britain's Greatest Defeat* (London, 2002), p. 60.

5 See, for example, A. Grayling, *Among the Dead Cities: Was the Allied Bombing of Civilians in WWII a Necessity or a Crime?* (London, 2005); J. Friedrich, *The Fire: The Bombing of Germany, 1940–1945* (New York, 2007).

WHAT BRITAIN HAS DONE

1939–1945

A Selection of Outstanding Facts and Figures

FOREWORD

The War Effort of Britain (the United Kingdom of Great Britain and Northern Ireland) is one important contribution to the common war effort of the United Nations. It is under this aspect that the British war effort is constantly viewed and operated. Such is the perspective of the outstanding facts and figures of Britain at war which are here presented. These facts are still not exhaustive, although much illuminating information has been made available in the White Paper (Cmd. 6564) presented by the Prime Minister to Parliament by Command of His Majesty on 28th November, 1944. Until the whole story can be told, the following selection is issued in the belief that it would be a grave disservice not only to Britain but also to her Allies in the common cause if an excessive reticence were to prevent a general understanding of what Britain has done in the Second World War.

Reference Division
Ministry of Information

9th May, 1945

R. 653

TABLE OF CONTENTS

I. THE ACHIEVEMENT OF BRITAIN AT WAR

'We must not underrate the gravity of the task which
lies before us or the temerity of the ordeal, to which we
shall not be found unequal. We must expect many
disappointments and many unpleasant surprises...
If these great trials were to come upon our island, there
is a generation of Britons here now ready to prove itself
not unworthy of the days of yore and not unworthy
of those great men, the fathers of our land, who laid the
foundations of our laws and shaped the greatness of
our country.'

RT HON. WINSTON CHURCHILL, 3rd September, 1939

Perspective

The policy of Britain in the world has for generations been
very largely directed in accordance with two constant tradi-
tions. The first of these has been the maintenance of
peaceful progress as far as possible in all quarters of the
globe. Between the two world wars Britain, as is notorious,
made sincere, prolonged and unavailing efforts to maintain
peace in the face of fascist provocation. But the second constant tradition of British policy is uttermost resistance to
attempts by any despotic aggressor to conquer and hold
down the continent of Europe. Britain has accordingly
fought necessary and successful wars against the domina-
tions of Louis XIV, Napoleon and Wilhelm II. In 1939 she
began to fight the domination of Hitler. In this war, as in the
previous one, Britain became the focus of a grand alliance

7

against aggression. Nor is her determination to resist aggression limited to Europe. The destruction of the Japanese militarism and the liberation of the peoples and territories which have fallen victims to its aggressive appetite are likewise in the forefront of British aims and policy.

Performance

Britain was the first nation in the world to go to war with Hitler's Germany without first being attacked herself.

Britain has been fighting Germany longer than any other nation except Poland.

Britain in 1940 saved the world from German domination by winning the Battle of Britain all but single-handed.

Britain's testing time in 1940–1 inspired her citizens to conduct which won the respect and admiration of the world.

Britain's total war effort per head of population is greater than that of any other belligerent.

Britain's strategy from 1940 onwards led up to total victory in Africa, to the redemption of the first whole continent from the enemy, and by preserving and developing Britain as the offensive base prepared the way for the invasion and liberation of the European continent.

Britain's campaigns in East and North Africa, culminating in the triumph in Tunisia, were among the most extensive and the most successful in all history.

Britain's sea power in the Mediterranean was a decisive factor in all the warfare against Italy, which achieved her unconditional surrender.

Britain's forces by their successful campaign in Burma have maintained for two years the largest land front against Japan.

Britain's sea power was the starting point and prime factor for the successful prosecution of the all-important Battle of the Atlantic, upon which the whole development of Anglo-American strategy depends. Britain's sea power made it possible to maintain the Arctic Convoys which have been carrying Aid to Russia since August 1941. Without sea power the 'glorious story' of the landings in North Africa, Sicily, Italy and France would not have been possible. The Battle of Normandy – 'the greatest and most decisive single battle of the entire war' – was followed by the offensives which carried the Allies to the frontiers of Germany, over the Rhine and into the heart of the Reich.

Britain has in this war raised the renown of her Royal Air Force to match that of her world-famous Royal Navy. The work of these two services on D-Day, coordinated with that of the armies they transported and protected, constitutes the greatest combined operation in history.

Britain has radically transformed her national existence by the extent of her mobilization for war.

Britain has been fanatical in stripping herself for war. No burden has been shirked, no sacrifice refused, no effort spared, no treasure stinted that might ensure or hasten ultimate victory, or tip the balance in a grim and bitterly contested struggle for freedom and very existence. The cost has been heavy, but has not been allowed to impede the British effort.

2. THE ACHIEVEMENT OF MANPOWER MOBILIZATION

'We shall not hesitate to take every step, even the most
drastic, to call forth from our people the last ounce and
the last inch of effort of which they are capable. The
interests of property, the hours of labour, are nothing
compared with the struggle for life and honour, for
right and freedom, to which we have vowed ourselves.'

RT HON. WINSTON CHURCHILL, 19th May, 1940

Perspective

Great Britain's population of effective working age (males
aged 14–64 and females aged 14–59) is relatively limited. At
30th June, 1944, it totalled 31,930,000. Of this figure 22
million had been mobilized by the same date.

The remaining 10 million consisted mainly of housewives with domestic responsibilities for war workers,
children, billetees, evacuees and invalids, and of students and
schoolchildren over fourteen, and invalids (including war
invalids).

British manpower mobilization has accordingly been
of the most stringent order. Of all the factors in war production manpower is particularly vital for Britain. It is also the
most stable, and Britain has had to make the maximum
effective use of her resources of manpower and good organization in order to make good destruction of plant, factories,
ports, railways, etc., by enemy action, and offset difficulties
in the import of raw materials, shortages, etc. Over and
above this, millions of British men and women have been

taken out of production for the armed and auxiliary services and for whole-time civil defence. Yet the total volume of production has been increased.

Performance

The magnitude of the task which the total mobilization of available manpower involved is shown by the fact that since the beginning of the war those responsible have had to deal with more than 30,000,000 registrations for national service of one kind or another.

Of the total figure of 15,910,000 males aged 14–64, 14,896,000 (or 93.6 per cent) had been mobilized in June 1944.

Of these, 4½ million were in the services, 225,000 in whole-time Civil Defence, 3,210,000 in the munitions industries, 4,059,000 in other essential work and 2,900,000 in other full-time employment.

The total of 4½ million men serving in the Armed Forces of the United Kingdom, compared with less than half a million at the beginning of the war, had been reached in spite of the casualties of five years of war. Including the number killed, missing, taken prisoner, or released on medical and other grounds, the total number of men who have served or are serving in the Armed Forces of the United Kingdom during this war is over 5½ million.

These men have been drawn mainly from the younger age groups. 57 per cent of all men between the ages of eighteen and forty have served or are still serving in the Armed Forces. The other men in these age groups have been retained in industry because of special skill, particularly in making munitions, or because they were unfit for service in the Armed Forces.

Those neither in the Services nor in whole-time Civil Defence, were giving additional service in their spare time –

1¾ million in the Home Guard, 1¼ million in part-time Civil Defence, and most of the remainder were performing forty-eight hours a month Fire Guard duties. These additional duties were obligatory for men who did less than sixty and women who did less than fifty-five hours a week in their employment.

Of the total of 16,020,000 women aged 14–59, 7,120,000 had been mobilized in June 1944.

Of these, 467,000 were in the Auxiliary Services, 56,000 in whole-time Civil Defence, 1,851,000 in the munitions industries, 1,644,000 in other essential work, and 3,102,000 in other full-time employment. The remainder were mainly housewives.

Some 900,000 were doing part-time work in industry (but have been included in the figures on the basis of two being equivalent to one whole-time worker) and 350,000 were doing part-time Civil Defence work.

Many others were doing war work in a variety of ways as members of salvage parties, collectors for Savings Groups, making and distributing hospital supplies, comforts for the Forces, and the Merchant Navy, etc.

Great Britain in 1941 was the first country to conscript women for the uniformed Auxiliary Services.

Of women in the 18–40 age groups, 90 per cent of the single women are working and over 80 per cent of the married women and widows without children.

Of women in the 18–50 age groups, 750,000 married women and widows with children and 2,000,000 without children are in paid employment.

Of single women in the 55–60 age group, 100,000 are in paid employment, excluding those in private domestic service.

At least 1,000,000 women of all ages are rendering voluntary service.

Women have played a magnificent part in freeing men for the forces or heavy industry.

In 1943, 40 per cent of the employees in the aircraft industry were women as compared with 12 per cent in 1940. In the engineering and allied industries the corresponding figures are 35 per cent in 1943 and 16 per cent in 1940.

About half of all the workers in the chemical and explosives industry are women.

In the munitions industries, including shipbuilding and heavy engineering, one worker in every three is a woman.

In agriculture and horticulture the introduction of 117,000 women has freed nearly 100,000 men; while 160,000 women have replaced 184,000 men in the various transport services.

Between June 1939 and June 1944 there was a net addition of 1,345,000 women in the munitions industries, 792,000 women in the basic industries and 523,000 women in the Auxiliary Services and whole-time Civil Defence.

Nearly three in every four British boys and girls between the ages of fourteen and seventeen are doing work in vital industry.

In order to achieve this mobilization of manpower the British have had to make many sacrifices and changes in the home life so dear to them. 22½ million removals of civilians alone have been recorded.

8,528,000 men and women workers are covered by Essential Work Orders. These Orders restrain workers in certain scheduled essential industries from leaving their employment and employers from dismissing them, except for serious misconduct, without the permission of a National Service Officer.

The needs of the Services have been met partly by

voluntary recruitment, but mainly by compulsory enlistment of men registered under the National Service Acts.

The compulsory enlistment of women in the Auxiliary Services was introduced in December 1941.

Compulsory registration for employment was also introduced in 1941.

Casualties have made severe inroads into the man-power available for the prosecution of the war. The total casualties (Armed Forces, Merchant Seamen and Civilians) sustained by the United Kingdom up to the beginning of May 1945 amounted to close on 1 million.

Of this total 746,109 were suffered by the Armed Forces (228,383 killed, 59,476 missing, 274,148 wounded and 184,102 prisoners of war). In spite of these losses the total strength of the Armed Forces increased each year since 1939.

During the same period 30,589 Merchant Seamen serving in British ships were killed by enemy action at sea and a further 12,993 were missing, wounded or interned by the enemy.

By the beginning of May 1945, the total of civilian casualties was 146,760. Of these 60,585 had been killed or died of injuries (including 25,392 women and 7,623 children) and 86,175 had been injured and detained in hospital. More than half (80,307) of the total civilian casualties occurred in the London region.

3. THE ACHIEVEMENT OF THE BRITISH ARMY

Perspective

British strategy was traditionally based upon a large navy and a relatively small army, which would form the framework for a systematic expansion to augment the great continental armies of her allies, in recent times France. But the fall of France at once threw the whole brunt of the war upon Britain at a time when the bulk of the Army's equipment had been lost at Dunkirk. Yet, even while Britain herself was imminently menaced by German invasion in 1940, the British Government took the bold and successful decision to send out important reinforcements to the Army of the Nile under General Wavell in accordance with long-term British strategy in the Mediterranean. The British Army was outnumbered by the enemy in every one of its campaigns in the first three years of war.

Performance

(a) Preliminary

> 'We shall not be content with a defensive war... We must put our defences in this island into such a high stage of organization that the fewest possible numbers will be required to give effective security and that the largest possible potential of offensive effort may be realised.'

> RT HON. WINSTON CHURCHILL, 4th June, 1940

'After more than five years of war we still maintain almost exactly the same number of divisions taking both theatres together (North-West Europe and Italy) in full action against the enemy as the United States have, by all the shipping resources which can be employed, yet been able to send to Europe. Considering that the population of the Empire of British race is only 70,000,000 and that we have sustained very heavy losses in the early years of the war, it certainly is a remarkable effort.'

RT HON. WINSTON CHURCHILL, 28th September, 1944

The British Army not only fought the enemy on the battle-fields of Europe, Africa and Asia, but also performed the key task of containing the enemy in strength by action in the British Isles, Iceland, Gibraltar, Malta, Cyprus, Palestine, Iraq, Syria, Persia, Madagascar, India.

1,600,000 British men joined the Home Guard as volunteers in less than two months from its formation in May 1940. Meantime the re-formed British Army was pacing into battle drill, the arduous and novel method of British military training which has produced such conspicuously successful results.

British Commando raids gained most valuable experience for the subsequent great amphibious attacks.

British resistance in Greece in the spring of 1941 seriously upset the German timetable and gained time which was of the first importance to our Russian allies.

The successful campaigns in Syria, Iraq and Persia in 1941 consolidated the very important Middle Eastern area against Axis designs and secured the supply lines by way of the Persian Gulf to Russia.

(b) Africa

*'One continent at least has been cleansed and purged for
ever from Fascist or Nazi tyranny.'*

RT HON. WINSTON CHURCHILL, 19th May, 1943

British armies conquered the whole extent of the great
Italian Empire in Africa with an area of 1,346,000 square
miles and a population of approximately 12,988,000. (These
armies of which the majority were composed of men from
the United Kingdom also included Australian, New
Zealand, South African and Indian Divisions.)

975,000 men was the total of Axis casualties in Africa.
More than 248,600 of these were Germans, and some
226,000 were natives serving in East Africa. The remainder
were Italians.

220,000 killed, wounded and missing were the total
casualties suffered by the forces of the British Empire in the
African and Middle Eastern theatres of war.

2,550 tanks, 6,200 guns and 70,000 lorries were captured or destroyed by British and Allied troops in all the
African campaigns.

In the East African campaign the forces under
Generals Cunningham and Platt in a few months conquered
Abyssinia – a powerfully defended country more than half as
large again as Germany. The first country to go under to
Axis aggression was the first to be freed.

British troops swiftly overran Italian East Africa, thus
greatly facilitating all later African successes, despite the fact
that at the start of the 1940 campaign the British forces in
the Sudan sector were outnumbered by almost ten to one.

In the East African campaign, in seventeen days (1st–
17th March, 1941) the columns under the command of
General Cunningham drove 744 miles from Mogadishu to

Jijga: an average of nearly 44 miles a day. This at the time was the fastest military pursuit in history. It was later approached by the onrush of the 8th Army in 1942–3, and was surpassed by that of the Guards Armoured Division through France and Belgium in 1944.

General Cunningham's troops in the East African campaign advanced in all 1,725 miles to Addis Ababa in fifty-three days – a staggering achievement.

250,000 men – the whole of an enemy army – were put out of action in the first North African campaign. Less than 2,000 casualties were suffered by the Army under Generals Wavell and Maitland Wilson.

In the final North African campaign the British 8th Army under Generals Alexander and Montgomery routed the Axis forces in the victorious Battle of Egypt fought at El Alamein, October–November 1942, which for the British Empire marked the turning point of the war, and was the first major defeat of the German armies in the field.

Over 86,000 casualties were inflicted upon the Germans and Italians when the British 8th Army drove the enemy out of Egypt and Libya. The enemy further lost about 500 tanks and 1,000 guns of all types.

The British 8th Army drove the German Afrika Korps 1,800 miles across North Africa.

The British 1st Army with its paratroops headed the Allied drive into Tunisia in November 1942.

The enemy armies in Tunisia were routed and completely destroyed, and their commander-in-chief taken prisoner, within less than one week from the opening of the final Allied offensive on 5th May, 1943.

At least 248,000 enemy prisoners and twenty-six generals were captured in Tunisia between 5th and 13th May, 1943. This constitutes one of the greatest defeats ever inflicted upon the German Army.

To achieve these victories in Africa before the reopening of the Mediterranean, sea voyages of over 12,000 miles were involved for the troops and supply ships. What this means can be judged by the fact that in order to transport the stores of one ordinary infantry division overseas seven ships of 10,000 tons each are required, carrying upwards of 200,000 packing cases.

The victorious pursuit by the 8th Army across North Africa was rendered possible by a triumph of British military administration. 120,000 lorries helped to carry the 2,400 tons of all stores which were supplied every day to the constantly advancing British troops. 2,000 new tyres were issued daily for these lorries.

76 per cent of the 8th Army and 90 per cent of the 1st Army in Tunisia were troops of the United Kingdom.

(c) Italy

> 'We have here in Italy one of the finest armies in the world. The combination of the Fifth Army and the British Eighth Army binds two veteran armies in a bond of brotherhood and comradeship of arms. No operation could have been more fruitful in this theatre than the work you have done in drawing away perhaps two dozen or more enemy divisions down into Italy where they have been torn to pieces.'

RT HON. WINSTON CHURCHILL, 21st August, 1944

The victories of the British arms were very largely responsible for the unconditional surrender of the kingdom of Italy in September 1943.

British Airborne troops headed the invasion of Sicily on 9th July, 1943, less than two months after the conquest of Tunisia.

The British 8th Army (including a Canadian Division), together with the American 7th Army, conquered the large island of Sicily in thirty-nine days (9th July–17th August, 1943).

About 167,000 of the enemy were killed, wounded or taken prisoner in the Sicilian campaign. This included 24,000 Germans killed and 128,000 Italians captured.

500 enemy guns, 260 tanks and 1,100 grounded aircraft were further captured by the Anglo-American forces in Sicily. The enemy lost 1,691 aircraft in all between 10th July and 17th August, 1943.

The British 8th Army led the assault upon the Fortress of Europe when they landed in Italy on 3rd September, 1943.

The landings of the Anglo-American 5th Army at Salerno and later at Anzio were, at the time, considered to be the most daring amphibious operations ever launched upon a similar scale in war.

On 11th May, 1944, General Alexander, Commander-in-Chief of all Allied Forces in Italy, launched the attack which broke through fortified German defence lines, and effected a junction of the main armies with the Anzio bridgehead forces. These brilliant moves and offensives which resulted in the liberation of Rome by forcing its abandonment by the enemy, without any destructive fighting within the city itself, were part of General Alexander's daring and original strategy.

By the middle of August 1944 the port of Ancona had been captured and the great city of Florence had been liberated by the British 8th Army. The 5th Army held the valuable port of Leghorn.

These operations during the summer and autumn of 1944 forced the Germans to employ up to thirty divisions. These divisions had lost a total of 194,000 in casualties –

equivalent to the total destruction of fifteen full-strength divisions.

In November 1944, General Alexander was promoted to the rank of Field Marshal (with effect from 4th June, the date of the liberation of Rome) in recognition of the brilliant strategy which had marked his conduct of the campaign – to end on 2nd May, 1945, with the surrender of 1,000,000 enemy troops.

The largest mass of all troops – in fact approximately half the number of divisions on the Italian front – has come from the United Kingdom.

(d) The Balkans

Early in 1943 a British Officer entered Yugoslavia by parachute, and was for eight months attached to Marshal Tito's headquarters. His mission was to advise the British Government on measures of help for Marshal Tito's partisans. In the autumn of 1943 a larger mission was established.

In the summer of 1944 units of British Land Forces Adriatic supported the partisans in operations against the Germans.

In October 1944, units of Land Forces Adriatic cleared the enemy from the islands of Naxos, Lemnos, Karpathos, Santorin, Chios, Mytilene and Samos.

By November 1944, as a result of the threat of the Red Army together with the successful operations of British Land Forces, Greece, aided by the Greek partisans, Athens and all the Greek mainland had been cleared of the enemy.

(e) Burma

'Along the Eastern Frontier of India stands the 14th British Imperial Army... This Army under Admiral

*Mountbatten, amounting to between 250,000 and
300,000 men apart from rearward services which in
that theatre of extraordinarily long and precarious
communications are very great, this Army has, by its
aggressive operation, guarded the pass of the American
air line to China and has protected India against the
horrors of a Japanese invasion... The ten Japanese
divisions that were launched against us with the object
of invading India have been repulsed and largely
shattered as the result of a bloody campaign... The
campaign of Admiral Mountbatten on the Burma
Frontier constitutes the largest and most important
ground fighting against the armies of Japan... It
constitutes the greatest collision which has yet taken
place on land with Japan and has resulted in the
slaughter of between 50,000 and 60,000 Japanese and
the capture of several hundred prisoners.'*

RT HON. WINSTON CHURCHILL, 28th August, 1944

On 25th August, 1943, Admiral Lord Louis Mountbatten
was appointed Supreme Allied Commander of the South
East Asia Command, in charge of land, sea and air operations against Japan in South East Asia.

The front on which the British are now fighting in
Burma extends some 700 miles and is second only in length
to the Russian Front. Burma is the hard land crust which
protects the Japanese conquests in China and South East
Asia. It is Japan's land route to India and, more importantly,
the Allies' land route to China. Both offensively and defen-
sively the Japanese have strained every nerve to hold it.

British and Indian troops of the 14th Army decisively
defeated the Japanese armies attempting to invade India.
The enemy committed over two-thirds of his forces in

Burma in this abortive attempt. The defence of Kohima by the mixed garrison which was there is one of the epic tales of the British and Indian Armies.

British and Indian troops of the Long Range Penetration Brigades, first under Major-General Wingate and later under Major-General Lentaigne, proved their ability to outfight the enemy in jungle warfare. They operated far behind the enemy lines, cutting his communications.

Perhaps the most striking single factor in the Burma campaign of 1943–4 was that, with the achievement of air superiority, the Allies were able to develop a new and highly effective form of jungle warfare, based on air transport and the dropping of supplies from the air. The operations of the Long Range Penetration Brigades depended entirely on aircraft for their transport and supply.

During the siege of Imphal, 2½ divisions were flown to Imphal and Dimapur to reinforce the garrisons there, and 30,000 non-combatant units flown out; in the month of June, a daily average of 700 tons of supplies was flown into Imphal.

By the end of 1944, the 14th Army had loosened the Japanese grip on the whole of Northern Burma. In March the land connection from India to China had been established, and by May 1945 Mandalay and Rangoon had been captured and the annihilation of Japanese Forces in Burma was proceeding rapidly, 97,000 Japanese having been killed and 250,000 casualties inflicted.

About one-third of the 14th Army were troops of the United Kingdom. In November 1944, its total strength including rearward services was given as 750,000 men. It formed more than three-quarters of all the Allied ground troops fighting in Burma.

(f) North-West Europe

'This is a glorious story, not only liberating the fields of France from atrocious enslavement but also uniting with bonds of true comradeship the great democracies of the West and the English-speaking peoples of the world.'

RT HON. WINSTON CHURCHILL, 2nd August, 1944

Preparations

Britain was the base from which the great Allied assault was launched on the continent of Europe.

Preparations for D-Day began in the early days of 1942. These plans, worked out to the last detail, have resulted in the brilliant victories that followed.

In April 1943, Lieutenant-General Morgan, of the British Army, was appointed chief of the joint planning staff which produced the plans for the Allied landings in Normandy, selected the beaches for the attack and presented the outline of the scheme together with a mass of detail to support it. At the Quebec Conference in August 1943 this plan received, in principle, complete agreement.

Large areas of territory along the coast of Britain were cleared in order to provide the many battle-training grounds required by both British and American forces.

The control and organization of equipment for the invasion forces took over a full year's work by the *Royal Army Ordnance Corps*.

The task of *waterproofing* all Allied invasion vehicles occupied the whole steel sheet capacity of the industries of Britain – 280 factories – for three months. Some 250 lorries were engaged for eight weeks in transporting the material from factories to RAOC depots; each lorry covered the ordinary mileage of a year in those two months. The RAOC had the task of receiving, assembling and issuing to the fighting units approximately half a million components of some 5,000 different types which the factories had produced in record time.

Before D-Day over 60,000,000 gallons of petrol had to be filled into containers in Britain. More than 500 special trains were required to move them to stores.

The *Royal Signals*, in collaboration with the staff of the *General Post Office*, planned and carried out a vast communications network, which involved 20,000 miles of high-grade circuits, provided as land-links for the extension of cross-Channel circuits to Service headquarters in this country.

The work of the *British Combined Operations Command*, founded in 1940 for the purpose of amphibious warfare, contributed greatly to the success of the Allied landings in France. The mass of knowledge accumulated from the British Commando raids on Lofoten, Spitzbergen, Vaagsö, Bruneval, St Nazaire and Dieppe were invaluable when planning the combined Allied assault on France.

The *Home Guard* of Britain assumed the operational responsibility of keeping watch and ward in the United Kingdom during the crossing of the Allied Expeditionary Force to France. They released many regular troops for employment on other tasks essential to the success of the operation, thus playing a decisive and integral part in the re-entry into France.

The *prefabricated harbour* (Mulberry) built in the sea off Arromanches ranks as one of the most imaginative pieces of war engineering in history.

Experts at the British Admiralty and War Office were responsible for the design and the construction of the components which formed the artificial harbour which was a triumph of British industry and labour. All the units were built entirely in Britain by British labour and with British materials.

As a result of the skill of British experts, craftsmen and seamen, the Allied Armies with all their vital supplies were put ashore in the most rapid build-up ever achieved in warfare, in spite of the worst June gale for forty years.

The prefabricated harbour made possible the liberation of Western Europe, not only by winning the battle of the build-up, but also by supplying and sustaining the advance from Falaise to the frontiers of Germany.

Operations

> *'The speed with which the mighty British and American armies in France were built up is almost incredible. In the first 24 hours a quarter of a million men were landed in the teeth of fortified and violent opposition. By the 20th day one million men were ashore… There are now between 2,000,000 and 3,000,000 men in France… I am glad to say that after 120 days of fighting we still bear in the cross-Channel troops a proportion of 2 to 3 in personnel and of 4 to 5½ fighting divisions in France.'*

RT HON. WINSTON CHURCHILL, 28th September, 1944

General Montgomery was Commander of all Allied ground forces under General Eisenhower up to 1st September, 1944, when he was promoted Field Marshal.

British, Canadian and American forces of the 21st Army Group carried out the initial assault on France. 'In the first stages of the invasion, the British and American forces were equal in size.' The British 6th Airborne Division together with British Commandos played the vital part in establishing the left flank of the Allied positions.

The experience of land–air cooperation, developed during the campaigns in North Africa, Sicily and Italy, was applied in the operations in North-West Europe, where the close integration of Army-Air Power has never been surpassed in the history of warfare.

The pinning down of the German armoured divisions by the British 2nd Army was the key to General Montgomery's strategy which led eventually to the capture of Cherbourg and to the eventual breakthrough by the American 3rd Army at the western end of the line. Mr Stimson, the US Secretary of War, paid tribute to the British and Canadian troops on the eastern sector 'for so engaging the enemy that he had no uncommitted strength with which to threaten the American corridor across the peninsula'.

The British and Canadians by containing seven out of ten German armoured divisions in the Caen-Falaise area contributed greatly to the destruction of the German armies. Of the German stand in the Caen area, General Eisenhower said that every foot of ground the Germans lost at Caen was like losing 10 miles anywhere else.

After the spectacular advance of the Guards Armoured Division from Flers to Brussels – 430 miles in nine days – they were again the spearhead of the British 2nd Army in the advance from Brussels to the Dutch Frontier and up to the German frontier near Nijmegen. On 3rd September they advanced 93 miles from Douai to Brussels. It was the longest and swiftest advance that any division of any nation has ever made in military history.

The British 1st Airborne Division was landed at Arnhem more than 50 miles behind the enemy's front line. General Eisenhower said that by fighting almost to extinction these airborne troops not only gave one of the most gallant examples of bravery, fortitude and courage in the history of warfare, but, by drawing to themselves all the fury of the German counter-attack, enabled the American 82nd and 101st Airborne Divisions to maintain their hold on the bridges behind them.

The operation at Arnhem was more than 85 per cent successful and the Allied Airborne invasion of Holland helped the military situation by driving a wedge 60 miles deep into a vital part of the enemy positions over flat country cut by canals.

Troops from the United Kingdom made up three-quarters of the Canadian 1st Army in the final campaign in North-West Europe, when it broke through the northern hinge of the enemy line covering the Rhine and turned the elaborate Siegfried defences.

When the time came for the final advance into Germany, the British 2nd Army forced the main Rhine crossing in the north against the determined and formidable opposition which the enemy had concentrated at a vital point, and broke through into the north German plain.

The dramatic culmination of a campaign which had carried 21st Army Group from the beaches of Normandy to the shores of the Baltic came on 5th May, 1945, with the unconditional surrender of the German armies in Holland, Denmark and North-West Germany to Field Marshal Montgomery. Over 1,000,000 Germans were involved.

4. THE ACHIEVEMENT OF THE ROYAL NAVY

Perspective

'It is upon the Navy, under the good providence of God,
that the wealth, safety and strength of the kingdom do
chiefly depend.'

Britain is an island. It follows that incoming supplies for the sustenance of the war effort must be brought by sea and that ships once again must carry the troops, equipment and stores required for the launching and maintenance of overseas campaigns. The ships which bear this inward and outward as well as coastwise traffic must be protected against relentless enemy attack by surface craft, U-boats and mines and aircraft across many thousands of miles of sea and ocean.

Britain is the key base for the Allied attack upon Germany. It was from this base that the Royal Navy's blockade of Germany and German-controlled Europe was mounted and maintained, the German fleet contained and ship by ship destroyed, and that enemy coastal convoys were sought out and attacked; that the African and Mediterranean campaigns were supplied and reinforced, and that innumerable combined operations were transported, landed and brought back. Finally it was from this base that, under the cover afforded by the Royal Navy and the RAF, the great armadas set forth which successfully accomplished the landings in North Africa and later the gigantic assault on North-West Europe.

All this and the escort of Arctic convoys to Russia have thrown an enormous strain on the men and ships of the Royal Navy who have had to spend long periods continuously at sea.

There has been a tremendous expansion in number both of ships and men in all branches of the service since the outbreak of war. New classes of vessels have been introduced.

In spite of having borne single-handed the whole burden of the war at sea for one and a half years after the loss of the French fleet to the Allies and before the United States entered the war, the Royal Navy has more than replaced the heavy losses it has inevitably sustained in the execution of its multifarious tasks and duties in all the seas and oceans.

As soon as the naval situation in the West permitted, a large and specially equipped Fleet was sent to the Pacific, in addition to the East Indies Fleet already operating in the Indian Ocean. The new British Pacific Fleet was in action by the end of March 1945.

Performance

I. CONVOY PROTECTION

(a) General

> '*We must regard the struggle at sea as the foundation of all the efforts of the United Nations. If they lost that, all else would be denied to them.*'

RT HON. WINSTON CHURCHILL, 8th September, 1942

More than 220,000 British and Allied vessels in 9,000 convoys were escorted to and from the United Kingdom and in surrounding waters between September 1939 and the end of 1944.

British ocean convoys in the same period totalled approximately 291,000,000 ship-miles. By 21st October, 1944, more than 350,000,000 tons of shipping had been convoyed across the Atlantic since the outbreak of war. Losses in convoy have steadily been reduced.

In 1941 one ship was lost out of every 181 which sailed in main North Atlantic and United Kingdom convoys; in 1942, one out of every 233; in 1943, one out of every 344. In the last half of 1943 losses in these convoys were less than one ship in 1,000. In the four months ended 18th September, 1943, no merchant vessel was sunk by enemy action in the North Atlantic. During the first fortnight in September 1943, no Allied ships were sunk by U-boat action in any part of the world. Losses continued to decrease in 1944.

On 21st October, 1944, it was disclosed that the largest supply convoy of all time – 167 ships, loaded with more than 1,000,000 tons of cargo, and covering an area of nearly 26 square miles – had recently crossed the Atlantic from North America and arrived in British ports without loss.

The Royal Navy, together with the Merchant Navy, saved the bulk of the British Expeditionary Forces in the evacuations from Norway, Dunkirk, Greece and Crete. And when the tide of war turned they played their part once more in landing the Allied Armies in Madagascar, North Africa, Sicily, Italy, Northern and Southern France and Greece.

The Royal Navy, from early 1940 until the summer of 1943, kept open, and constantly convoyed reinforcements to the Middle East by, the long Cape Route. This is a voyage of 12,000 miles; that to India is about the same.

During the year ended 31st July, 1944, British ships brought to the United Kingdom some 865,000 uniformed Americans; of these 320,500 were carried in the great liners *Queen Mary* and *Queen Elizabeth* which have steamed nearly a million miles and carried 1,250,000 troops during the war. The safety of their passage depended upon the Royal Navy and Allied command of the seas.

By October 1944, out of 10,600,000 soldiers who had been moved all over the world in our troop convoys, only 2,978 had lost their lives through enemy action at sea.

Convoys escorted by the Royal Navy, at great risk, to Malta and to Russia did much towards tiding the Allies over difficult periods in the parallel campaigns in Russia and North Africa and building up their power to hit back.

The round trip from the north of England to Archangel and back is about 6,000 miles counting deviations. This lies mainly within the Arctic Circle, between the pack ice and the enemy air and U-boat bases.

By March 1945, since the commencement of these Russian convoys sixteen British warships had been sunk on this duty, and in some periods there were very considerable losses of merchant ships. Yet, over all, 677 cargo ships and approximately 90 per cent of the cargoes consigned got through. Nearly 900 of HM ships and approximately 260,000 men were involved in convoy escorts to Russia.

The work of convoy, patrolling and shipping protection involves great strain on men and ships alike, and some of them stay at sea for periods undreamed of in pre-war days.

HMS *Cumberland* was at sea for 206 days out of a total of 213 from November, 1940; and from the outbreak of war up to 23rd February, 1943, this ship had steamed nearly a quarter of a million miles.

Between September 1939 and February 1943, HM

Destroyer *Forester* steamed 200,000 miles, a distance equal to nine times round the world.

In a single year the corvette *Jonquil* steamed a distance equivalent to more than three times round the world.

In one year and four months HM Destroyer *Wolfhound* steamed over 50,000 miles and convoyed 3,000 ships.

From her commissioning in 1940 up to July 1944, HM Destroyer *Havelock* steamed 300,000 miles.

Over the whole of the huge mass of shipping which entered the Mediterranean between 8th November, 1942, and 8th May, 1943, losses were less than 2¼ per cent, or nine ships out of every 400.

In one year, from 4th October, 1943, to 4th October, 1944, 270 convoys of 3,700 merchant vessels of all types, of 25,104,067 gross tons, sailed from Naples and its satellite ports, together with 1,351 schooners engaged in inter-coastal trade. These figures exclude all Allied warships, together with all landing craft engaged on the regular shuttle service to Anzio between January and June 1944, and more recently for the supply of the Army and Air Force through Civita Vecchia, Piombino and Livorno.

(b) Anti-Submarine Warfare

> *'There will not be in this war any period when the seas will be completely safe but neither will there be, I believe, any period when the full necessary traffic of the Allies cannot be carried on. We shall suffer and we shall suffer continuously, but by perseverance, and by taking measures on the largest scale, I feel no doubt that in the end we shall break their hearts.'*

RT HON. WINSTON CHURCHILL, 8th November, 1939

In May 1943, for the first time, the killings of U-boats substantially outnumbered their output.

From August to November 1943, more U-boats were sunk than Allied ships were destroyed by U-boat action.

The number of U-boats sunk during the war had, by 8th May, 1945, exceeded 700 of which over 500 were accounted for by British Empire forces.

In two months during the invasion of Northern France seventeen U-boats were sunk while attempting to interfere with Allied cross-Channel traffic. In spite of this, however, in the first month of the operations, though thousands of Allied ships were moved across the Channel and coastwise to build up the vast forces on the continent, no merchant vessel of that great concourse was sunk by U-boat; with the possible exception of one ship, which might equally have struck a mine.

The U-boat war, however, demands unceasing attention. Only the zeal and vigour of the Allied air and surface forces have procured the comparative safety of their shipping and the enemy's scant success.

(c) Minesweeping

> *'There are deliverances which we should never forget. There was the mining peril, the sea mining peril, which loomed so large in 1939 and which has been mastered by superior science and ingenuity and by the often forgotten but almost unsurpassed devotion to duty of our minesweeping crews and of the thousand ships they work and man that we may eat and live and thus fight for the good cause.'*

RT HON. WINSTON CHURCHILL, 22nd February, 1944

The Minesweepers of the Royal Navy have played a most vital part in the safe arrival of convoys in all parts of the world. 20,000 mines have been swept in the coastal waters round Britain, in the Channel and North Sea, in the Mediterranean, in the Cape area and round the coasts of India and Australia.

By June 1943, the number of mines destroyed in the swept channels would have been sufficient, if each one had been lethal, to destroy the whole British merchant fleet two and a half times over.

To clear the Sicilian Channel and open the Mediterranean so as to reduce the distance between Britain and Egypt by 9,000 miles, the 12th and 13th Minesweeping Flotillas of the Royal Navy each steamed 2,500 miles. They swept a channel of 600 square miles. In the course of this operation, which took a month, 257 mines were swept.

In all, about 4,000 mines of all descriptions were swept or destroyed by Allied Minesweepers in the Mediterranean, including the Ægean, during 1944.

HM Minesweeper *Bay*'s crew claim that the *Bay* has sailed through the Straits of Dover more often than any other ship during the war. In early 1944 she swept her 240th convoy through and steamed her 20,000th mile.

BYMS 2002, senior ship of the 150th Minesweeping Flotilla, has steamed 35,000 miles since her launching in March 1942. This flotilla destroyed 130 mines in the course of recent operations and one sweep, yielding twenty-two mines, occupied fifteen days, without any of the men of the flotilla going ashore.

II. OFFENSIVE ACTIONS

'The spirit of all our forces serving on salt water has never been more strong and high than now. The

warrior heroes of the past may look down, as Nelson's monument looks down on us now, without any feeling that the island race has lost its daring or that the examples they set in bygone centuries have faded as the generations have succeeded one another.'

RT HON. WINSTON CHURCHILL, 22nd February, 1944

(a) Enemy Losses

During the fifty-two months of war up to 31st December, 1943, a total of 10,056,000 gross tons of enemy shipping was captured, sunk or damaged by surface ships, sub-marines, aircraft or mines; more than 2,515,000 of which was sunk, captured or damaged during 1943 alone. (Losses inflicted on Japanese shipping and by Russian forces are not included.)

By May 1942, apart from operations in the Far East, 86 per cent of the German and Italian surface warships so far destroyed, damaged or captured; 89 per cent of all enemy merchant ships put out of action; and 94 per cent of the enemy submarines destroyed by the Allies were sunk by United Kingdom forces.

Since the outbreak of war well over 150 German naval surface craft of all types, and over 130 Italian (excluding those probably sunk) have been sunk by British naval or naval air action.

Continuing throughout 1944 the offensive which they have maintained unremittingly since the first hour of the war, HM Submarines sank during the year at least 400 enemy ships of various sizes, ranging from coastal ammuni-tion runners to large troop ships, tankers and merchant vessels. They also sank more than twenty-three Axis war-ships, including two cruisers, one of which was blown up by a human torpedo.

Up to 31st July, 1944, the number of enemy aircraft show down by HM Ships was 674 confirmed, 222 probably destroyed and 330 damaged. During the same period naval aircraft destroyed 266, probably destroyed 44 and damaged 165.

From the outbreak of war up to 31st December, 1943, Light Coastal Forces of the Royal Navy had destroyed well over 100 enemy ships and by May 1943 they were averaging one action per night. This pace has been kept up throughout 1944 in all areas. During the year 1944 in the Mediterranean theatre alone Light Coastal Forces destroyed a total of seventy-six enemy vessels, including a number of E-boats and other escorts and thirty-three supply ships.

(b) Mediterranean

In the Mediterranean the Royal Navy in spite of numerical inferiority won every major action, including the great naval air attack on Taranto Harbour, and the historic Battle of Cape Matapan.

Not one British warship was sunk by an Italian surface vessel during the three years and more that Italy was at war with Britain.

In the seven months following the occupation of French North Africa, submarines in the Western Mediterranean sank 430,000 tons of enemy shipping and damaged 70,000 tons. Allied surface forces sank, or captured, 28 merchant vessels totalling 60,000 tons, 5 destroyers, 2 torpedo-boats and many smaller craft.

1,000,000 tons of Axis shipping had been sunk by British submarines in the Mediterranean by 23rd January, 1943.

The victory of the British Fleet over the Italian was completed by the unconditional surrender of Italy. By November 1943, the following ships of the Italian Navy

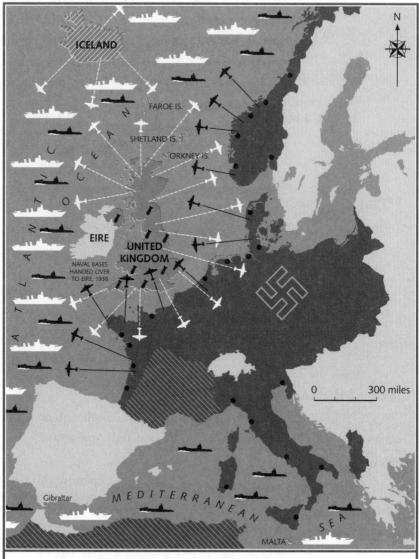

BLOCKADE AND COUNTER-BLOCKADE, 1940

By her march to the Atlantic, Germany hoped to break the British blockade of the Continent of Europe and to establish a counter-blockade of the British Isles. But the blockade against supplies to Germany was maintained, while the long and bloody battles fought by civilians, seamen and airmen, kept open the sea routes to and from Britain, preserved the offensive base, and made certain the defeat of Germany.

| BRITISH TERRITORY | BRITISH BASES | ENEMY AND ENEMY-HELD TERRITORY | VICHY FRANCE | NEUTRAL TERRITORY | COUNTER-BLOCKADE BY BOMBING | BRITISH AIR PATROLS | BRITISH SURFACE BLOCKADE | U-BOAT COUNTER-BLOCKADE | ENEMY AIR ATTACKS | U-BOAT BASES |

Map labels: ICELAND · FAROE IS. · SHETLAND IS. · ORKNEY IS. · EIRE · UNITED KINGDOM · NAVAL BASES HANDED OVER TO EIRE, 1938 · ATLANTIC OCEAN · Gibraltar · MEDITERRANEAN SEA · MALTA · N · 0 300 miles

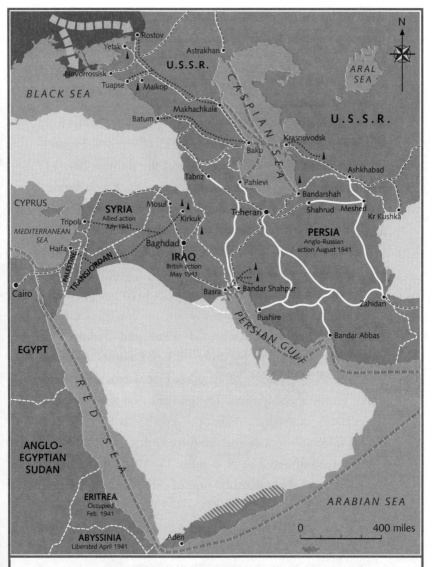

N

ARAL
SEA

Rostov
Yetsk
Astrakhan
U.S.S.R.
Novorrossisk
Tuapse · Maikop
BLACK SEA
Makhachkala
Batum
U.S.S.R.
Krasnovodsk
Baku
Ashkhabad
Tabriz
Pahlevi
Bandarshah
CYPRUS
Mosul
Kirkuk
Teheran
Shahrud Meshed
Kr Kushka
Tripoli
SYRIA
Allied action
July 1941
PERSIA
Anglo-Russian
action August 1941
MEDITERRANEAN
SEA
Haifa
PALESTINE
Baghdad
TRANSJORDAN
IRAQ
British action
May 1941
Basra · Bandar Shahpur
Cairo
Zahidan
Bushire
EGYPT
Bandar Abbas
PERSIAN GULF
ANGLO-
EGYPTIAN
SUDAN
RED SEA
ARABIAN SEA
ERITREA
Occupied
Feb. 1941
0   400 miles
ABYSSINIA
Liberated April 1941
Aden

SECURING THE MIDDLE EAST, 1941–2

In 1941 Axis schemes forced the Allies to look to the security of the Middle East.
In May pro-Axis plots in Iraq were defeated by British action, in July Vichy influence
was expunged from Syria and the Lebanon by an Anglo-French force, and in
August joint Russo-British action, with the co-operation of the new Persian regime,
ensured the safety of the Persian routes. Thus the oil of the Middle East was secured
to the Allies, the development of the Southern Route to Russia was assured, and the
possibilities of joint German and Japanese machinations were forestalled.

BRITISH AND ALLIED TERRITORY   ENEMY-HELD   NEUTRAL   SUPPLY   ROADS   RAILWAYS   OIL PIPE LINE   ENEMY
AND BASES   TERRITORY   TERRITORY   LINES   AND OIL FIELDS   ADVANCE

were under Allied control; 5 battleships, 8 light cruisers, 31 destroyers and torpedo-boats, 40 submarines and scores of smaller craft.

A task force of British escort aircraft carriers operated with much success in the Mediterranean in the summer of 1944. In nine days off the Riviera in September aircraft from this force flew a total distance of 275,605 miles. Fighter-bombers went out on 532 sorties and the fighters flew 119 sorties in spotting for naval bombardment, 84 on tactical reconnaissance, 114 on providing cover for the beaches, and 132 providing fighter cover over the task group.

In September 1944, British and Allied warships began a campaign in the Ægean which speedily brought about the destruction or capture of all German or German controlled shipping in the area. The islands of Naxos, Lemnos, Karpathos, Santorin, Chios, Mytilene and Samos were cleared of the enemy by units of Land Forces Adriatic, leaving only the islands of Rhodes, Cos, Leros and Melos under German occupation. The garrisons on these remaining islands – equivalent to about two divisions – we virtually cut off from all supplies and reinforcements.

It was estimated in November 1944 that the past year the enemy lost about 100,000 tons of shipping in the Ægean of an available total of 110,000 tons. Of these, 40,000 tons were destroyed by surface vessels, naval aircraft and submarines; 33,000 by shore-based aircraft and 24,000 scuttled by the enemy to avoid capture. Between 9th September and 27th October, Admiral Troubridge's fleet sank thirty-one enemy warships and transports of various sizes and forty small craft. In addition sixteen warships and merchant ships and at least fifteen small craft were severely damaged; naval aircraft attacked targets on the islands and on the mainland, bombardments were carried out, troops landed, and three islands surrendered to HM Ships.

(c) Naval Support for Land Operations in the Mediterranean

The Royal Navy has rendered possible the great amphibious assaults of the Allies in African and Mediterranean waters. It was primarily responsible for the highly successful landings of Allied forces in French North Africa, and subsequently in Sicily, Italy and Southern France.

850 ships, including 350 warships of all sizes, were engaged in the Anglo-American amphibious operation against French North Africa. Two out of the three major convoys sailed from Britain under the protection of the Royal Navy and Royal Air Force. Not a single life or ship was lost on the way.

3,000 ships of all kinds and sizes were engaged in the Anglo-American attack upon Sicily. In the initial assault 160,000 men, 14,000 vehicles, 600 tanks and 1,800 guns were transported.

The part played by naval gunnery in the assault upon Salerno in September 1943, during which the naval guns turned the tide of battle in the Allies' favour, is but one example of the development of the use of warships as floating batteries for tactical cooperation with land forces.

During the critical period between 9th and 12th September between 6,000 and 10,000 shells of all calibres were being fired daily at targets in the Salerno area.

During the Sicilian campaign the Royal Navy subjected the island to more than fifty organized bombardments, and fired more than 20,000 rounds against selected enemy targets.

In the naval bombardment prior to the landings on the French Riviera in August 1944, 15,900 shells, of which 12,500 were of over 12-inch calibre, were fired. The naval force operating in this area was estimated to comprise roughly 50 per cent British ships.

(d) Actions in North European and Atlantic Waters (See also North-West Europe)

British warships with few opportunities have scored notable successes against the German fleet; including the sinking of the battleships *Graf Spee* (13th–17th December, 1939), *Bismarck* (23rd–27th May, 1941), and the *Scharnhorst* (26th December, 1943); and such actions as the destruction of three out of a force of eleven destroyers (without loss) by two of HM Cruisers in the Bay of Biscay on 27th and 28th December, 1943.

During the Norwegian campaign two major naval engagements took place in Narvik Fjord (10th and 13th April, 1940). As a result eleven German destroyers, six supply ships and an ammunition vessel were sunk, and two destroyers severely damaged, for the loss of two British destroyers, and damage to several others.

In September 1943, British midget submarines delivered an attack of the utmost daring and damaged the German battleship *Tirpitz* in her very anchorage deep in Alten Fjord, Northern Norway. This was the first employment of British midget submarines.

The *Tirpitz* was subsequently attacked successfully by naval Barracuda aircraft in April and again in August 1944. The attack on this ship was maintained in September with an assault by Russia-based Lancasters of the Royal Air Force. In October, the damaged ship was being moved from her anchorage in Kaa Fjord, and on 29th October she was again attacked by the RAF west of Tromsö.

The *Tirpitz* was finally sunk in Tromsö Fjord on 12th November in an attack by two squadrons of Lancasters of RAF Bomber Command. This action left Germany with no modern battleship that was operational and thus released British battleships for duties in the Far East.

> *'These operations were protected and supported by a considerable British Fleet assisted by a strong detachment of the American Fleet, the whole under Admiral Ramsay. In spite of gales, in spite of mines, in spite of more than 100 German submarines waiting, baffled, in the Biscay ports, and a swarm of E-boats and other marauders, ceaseless traffic has been maintained over the 100-mile stretch of Channel, and General Eisenhower, with his lieutenant, General Montgomery, now stands at the head of a very large and powerful army, equipped as no army has ever been equipped before.'*

RT HON. WINSTON CHURCHILL, 2nd August, 1944

In the initial assault there were 5,143 ships and craft, of which 4,226 were landing ships and landing craft. Of the great fleet of warships over twenty were cruisers, and battleships, seven of them, operated in the restricted waters of the Channel within range of enemy shore batteries.

During the first four weeks of the continental campaign no fewer than 1,000,000 men, 183,500 vehicles, and 650,000 tons of stores were landed in Normandy. During this period the average daily number of convoys going across the Channel was sixteen.

Forerunners of the great armada were 200 minesweepers, manned by 10,000 officers and men, and carrying 2,800 tons of sweeping material. The oropesa sweepers, sweeping for moored mines alone, carried 70 miles of wire. 80 per cent of these vessels were British.

Between 6th June and 31st December, in the assault and subsequent operations east and west of the Seine Bay, over 1,700 mines were swept. Admiral Sir Bertram Ramsay said that in the first three months of the North-West European campaign (6th June–6th August) the total number of mines swept by Allied ships represented 10 per cent of the mines swept in all theatres, during five years of war.

After the minesweepers went the bombarding warships, bringing 800 guns (from 16-inch to 4-inch) to bear on the enemy. 2,000 tons of shells were fired in the first ten minutes, 22,000 in the first ten days.

By noon on D-Day HMS *Warspite* alone had fired 175 rounds of 15-inch ammunition, amounting to some 150 tons.

The guns of the Fleet supported the Allied Armies until targets were too far inland to be within range, though the battleships engaged with accuracy at anything up to 30,000 yards. On one occasion a cruiser's guns were used in support of British infantry faced by a force of German Tiger tanks. The range was 20,000 yards, the leading Tigers were within 300 yards of the British infantry, but the cruiser's shells fell right among the enemy who were routed.

In ten days of bombardment to help break up enemy concentrations massing around Caen, HMS *Ramillies* fired over 1,000 rounds of 15-inch and 6-inch ammunition.

During the assault upon the strongly fortified island of Walcheren, in the Scheldt Estuary, HMS *Warspite*, and HM monitors *Erebus* and *Roberts*, bombarded the enemy positions at a fairly long range while small close support craft, manned by Royal Marines, pressed inshore to fire at point-blank range, affording magnificent support to the heavily opposed landings. Owing to weather conditions these operations had to be carried out without air support and very heavy losses were suffered among the landing and close support craft. But in spite of this the shore batteries were neutralized, which permitted the troops to gain a foothold, and the minesweepers to enter the estuary; thus was the vital port of Antwerp opened to Allied supply ships.

During the seven months from D-Day to the end of the year, over 140,000 rounds had been fired by Allied warships in general support of military operations and over 8,000 in the bombardment of specified targets.

More than fifty British warships, destroyers, frigates, and smaller craft, were constantly employed in the duty of screening and protecting convoys and bombarding warships, of patrolling against enemy attack and attacking the enemy convoys. They ranged over a sea area of 300 square miles and were involved in many actions, achieving some outstanding successes.

Most of the burden of the battle of the Channel in the first stages of the invasion of North-West Europe fell upon the light coastal forces of the Royal Navy. In fourteen days in August, coastal force units carried out 145 sorties and covered 28,600 miles. And in one week nineteen enemy ships were sunk, three driven ashore and twenty-eight damaged.

From 6th June to the end of 1944, sixty-eight enemy ships and vessels from destroyers to small merchantmen were destroyed in operations carried out by the Royal Navy with the addition of Canadian and Polish destroyers and other Allied coastal craft, from the mouth of the Gironde in the west to Den Helder in the east.

During the campaign in France much fine work was done by Obstacle Clearance and Harbour Recovery units. In three days an Obstacle Clearance Unit had made 2 miles of beach safe by the detonation of 2,400 mines and other obstacles and from June to December 1944, eight large ports were made serviceable by the work of the minesweepers and harbour recovery parties.

The Admiralty, in conjunction with the War Office, undertook the movement of the components of the prefabricated harbours to their assembly parks in the United Kingdom, the sinking of the caissons in the harbours, and the construction of the piers.

The Admiralty was responsible for the block ships, the floating breakwaters and the conformity of the caisson design with naval requirements as regards towing and seaworthiness, and for the final location of the equipment in the assembly parks. The Navy was also responsible for towing the equipment across the Channel; though the general layout of the artificial harbours was a joint Admiralty and War Office responsibility.

This was an immense achievement, and when the first harbour was completed many thousands of tons of vital war material were unloaded each day. Even on the worst day of the worst June gale for forty years, 800 tons of petrol and ammunition as well as many troops were landed over the piers.

In conjunction with the landings in Normandy, an extensive series of mine-laying operations were carried out in enemy waters by minelayers of the Royal Navy, with aircraft of the RAF. By 17th October, it was evident that over 100 enemy warships, auxiliaries and merchant vessels were sunk or severely damaged by British mines, 30 per cent of which losses were attributable to mines laid by naval forces.

Without Britain's Navy, her Merchant Navy, and her command of the seas, the invasion of Europe would have been impossible. It was made possible by the winning of the Battle of the Atlantic, by the defeat of the U-boat, by mastering the mine menace, and by putting the German battle fleet out of action.

(f) The Far East

*'For a year past, our modern battleships have been
undergoing a further measure of modernisation and
tropicalisation to meet the rapid war–time changes in
technical apparatus. We had already, nine months ago,
begun the creation of an immense fleet train… in order
that our Fleet may have a degree of mobility which for
several months together will make them largely
independent of shore bases.'*

RT HON. WINSTON CHURCHILL, 28th September, 1944

In August 1944, the First Lord of the Admiralty disclosed
that already 85 per cent of the work done in the Indian
Ocean was being carried out by the Royal Navy.

In November 1944, Admiral Sir James Somerville,
head of the British Admiralty Delegation in Washington,
announced that approximately 2,000,000 tons of shipping
are now at sea in the Indian Ocean at any given time.

In the year 1944 alone, HM Submarines operating in
Far Eastern waters had sunk one Japanese cruiser and 157
other ships, ranging from large supply vessels to anti-sub-
marine craft. A Japanese aircraft carrier was hit by torpedo
and believed to have been sunk; and another Japanese cruiser
was hit by torpedo.

As well as the successful British submarines in the Far
East, and the Light Coastal Forces operating off Burma, a
substantial number of larger units of the British Eastern
Fleet, including battleships and aircraft carriers, operated
with much success in the Andaman and Nicobar Islands and
Netherlands East Indies areas during 1944.

Units of the Royal Navy have also attacked Japanese
rail communications in bombardments of the coast of the

Malay Peninsula, and raids have been carried out by Royal Marine Commandos in this area.

In December 1944, the formation of two British eastern fleets instead of one was announced. These were the British Pacific Fleet, based on Australia, under Admiral Sir Bruce Fraser, and the East Indies Fleet, based on Ceylon, under Admiral Sir Arthur Power.

III. CASUALITIES

The Prime Minister announced on 22nd February, 1944, that 'the total of personnel, officers and men of the Royal Navy lost since the war started is just over 30 per cent of its pre-war strength, the figures being 41,000 killed out of 133,000, which was the total strength at the outbreak of war', and which had multiplied many times since then. At the end of 1944 figures for naval casualties had amounted to 47,000 men killed or missing, 13,000 wounded, and 5,500 in prison camps.

The loss of ships, though heavy, had been more than replaced by new construction. Losses amount to 5 battle-ships and battle-cruisers, 8 aircraft carriers, 28 cruisers, 128 destroyers, 77 submarines and 52 sloops, frigates and corvettes.

5. THE ACHIEVEMENT OF THE MERCHANT NAVY

Perspective

Before the Second World War, Britain's Merchant Fleet was the largest in the world, with a gross tonnage of about 17,500,000 tons (not including 3,000,000 tons of Dominion shipping); though even then UK tonnage was about one million tons smaller than it had been before the First World War. A very great strain was imposed upon the ships and the seamen in order to master the usual perils of the sea, as well as a strong and unscrupulous enemy, and maintain the supply of vital raw materials and foodstuffs without which the people of Britain could neither fight nor live. From the start, however, Britain applied her great experience in the organization of coastal and ocean convoys, and her merchant seamen have maintained not only the British base, but the various fronts and garrisons established throughout the world, carrying aid also to Russia and playing an indispensable part in the combined operations which resulted in the successful landings in North Africa, Sicily, Salerno and France.

Performance

> 'Without your devoted service, there could be no victory
> for our arms. From the Master in command, to the boy
> on his first voyage, you have worked together with the
> steady discipline of free men who know what is at

*stake. Your reward is the consciousness of duty done and
the affection and respect of all your countrymen.'*

HIS MAJESTY THE KING, 25th December, 1943

*'The Merchant Navy, with Allied comrades, night and
day, in weather fair or foul, face not only the ordinary
perils of the sea but the sudden assaults of war from
beneath the waters or from the sky... We are a seafaring
race, and we understand the call of the sea... We feel
confident that that proud tradition of our island will be
upheld to-day wherever the ensign of a British
merchantman is flown.'*

RT HON. WINSTON CHURCHILL, 31st July, 1941

Over 2,000 merchant ships from the United Kingdom are at
sea at any time.

It is to the ships and men of the Merchant Navy (as
well as the Royal Navy) that hundreds of thousands of men
of the Forces owe their lives and freedom after the evacuations from Norway, Dunkirk, Greece and Crete, and to the
Merchant Navy that much of the credit must go for the successful landing and subsequent maintenance of the Allied
Forces in North Africa, Sicily, Italy, North and South
France.

In the first six months of war about 1,900 merchant
vessels were armed, and during the first year nearly 3,000. By
the beginning of February 1943, 8,300 British and Allied
merchant ships had been fitted with guns and other devices
for their defence.

Fishing vessels and ships of the Merchant Navy alone
had shot down 141 enemy aircraft, from 12th April, 1940, to
the end of July 1944; and had shared, with HM ships, the
shooting down of a further 163 during the same period.

The tanker *British Confidence* steamed 243,000 miles in the first four years of war. Some of the large motor ships with a high speed have completed 300,000 miles in the same period.

Another tanker, the *British Judge*, steamed 20,000 miles with a hole as large as a medium-sized house in her side. This occurred in the Far East and she had to be taken by devious ways to Mobile, Alabama, for her extensive repairs.

23,000 military vehicles, some 1,300 aircraft, over 400,000 tons of military and air stores, and hundreds of locomotives were carried overseas by United Kingdom shipping in the single month of October 1941.

300 ships were continuously employed during 1941 on the 12,000 mile voyage round the Cape to support British armies in the Middle East.

500,000 men, 50,000 tanks and other vehicles, and 1,000,000 tons of stores, were carried round the Cape to destinations in the Middle East, India and the Far East, during 1942.

Over 3,000,000 tons of military stores, including 1,000,000 tons of food, had been landed in Egyptian ports up to April 1942.

12,000 ships carrying over 77,000,000 tons of cargo had been convoyed from Canadian shores up to the middle of June 1943.

500,000 men and over 1,000,000 tons of stores were landed in North Africa in the first four months of the Tunisian campaign.

During the six months of the Tunisian campaign more than 1,000 merchant ships left the United Kingdom carrying a constant stream of millions of tons of supplies to the armies in North Africa.

*

On 6th June, 1944, when 1,000 merchant vessels, manned by 50,000 seamen, crossed the Channel to Normandy, the Merchant Navy redeemed the promise it made as its ships left Norway, Dunkirk, Greece and Crete.

These ships had to be considered individually two years beforehand as to their suitability for the carriage of various types of cargo. The immense fleet had to be assembled, loaded, and finally convoyed across the Channel with its vital cargoes.

In the first three days following 6th June, thirty-eight convoys had to get to France – some of from 90 to 100 ships. Nearly 750 of the major types of vessels were in these thirty-eight convoys, excluding escorts.

It says much for the strength of Britain's Merchant Fleet that this colossal operation could be undertaken, and kept supplied and reinforced, while convoys still sailed across the Atlantic, in the Far North, and to supply the Allied Armies in the Mediterranean.

It is by the ships of the Merchant Navy that the three-quarter million items in the range of the Army's fighting and technical stores and the three-quarter million items in the RAF's stores are moved.

Approximately 100,000 tons of shipping a year are required to transport a division of 20,000 men 1,000 miles overseas, with arms, equipment and stores, and to keep it supplied and reinforced.

16½ tons of spare parts must, it is estimated, be shipped overseas in order to keep 100 25-pounder guns in action for one year. One medium tank may need up to 2 tons of spare parts in a year.

Every bomber sent overseas requires, it is calculated, a total of 1,000 tons of shipping space to carry the personnel, petrol, bombs and spare parts necessary to put it into operation. All these have to be carried by ships.

One of the boldest achievements of the Merchant Navy was the maintenance throughout the winter of 1943–4 of a service by sea between Sweden and Britain. A fleet of small, powerful vessels successfully ran the German blockade in the Skagerrak, transporting valuable cargoes and carrying the Red Ensign into Swedish waters for the first time in three and a half years.

There have been many individual acts of bravery in Britain's Merchant Navy, and from the outbreak of war up to 31st December, 1944, more than 6,300 ship-masters, officers and men had received awards.

During five and a half years of war 30,589 Merchant seamen in British ships lost their lives, 4,215 were wounded, 690 missing, and a further 4,088 were interned by the enemy.

In February 1944, Mr Churchill said that since the beginning of the war the proportion of Merchant seamen hailing from the British Isles alone who have been lost at sea on their vital duty, has been about one-fifth of the average number engaged in this service.

The loss of Merchant ships has been equally heavy. By 8th May, 1945, 2,570 British ships of nearly 11½ million gross tons had been lost. Though these losses were partly offset by new construction, purchase and organization, the British ocean-going Merchant Fleet had been reduced to 13½ million gross tons at the end of 1943. The situation, however, improved in 1944.

6. THE ACHIEVEMENT OF THE ROYAL AIR FORCE

Perspective

At the outbreak of war the Royal Air Force was much smaller than the Luftwaffe, prepared as it was for aggression. But the Royal Air Force was of the highest quality. The victory of British fighters in the Battle of Britain was a victory, not only for British fighting prowess but also for British scientific technique and foresight. Similar foresight developed the heavy bombers and, in 1939, initiated the great Commonwealth Air Training Plan, to provide the crews to man the bombers. Thus, after Fighter Command had saved Britain from German invasion in 1940, Bomber Command was able to launch an ever-mounting aerial offensive against the industrial centres of the Reich, thereby depriving the enemy of the opportunity to build up his reserves, compelling him to divert aircraft from the battle fronts for home defence, to such an extent as to leave his armies without adequate air cover. At the same time, units of the RAF operating with Allied armies in North Africa, Sicily, Italy, North-West Europe, the Balkans, Eastern Mediterranean, India and Burma have led the way to new heights of land–air cooperation. Meanwhile, and all the time, a greatly strengthened Coastal Command has played a decisive part in defeating the U-boat menace.

Performance

(a) Fighter Operations

> *'Never in the field of human conflict was so much owed by so many to so few.'*
>
> RT HON. WINSTON CHURCHILL, 20th August, 1940

The Royal Air Force decisively defeated the Luftwaffe in the Battle of Britain. On five separate occasions during August–September 1940, over 100 enemy aircraft were shot down in a single day; on 15th August, 181 were destroyed, and on 15th September, 185. During the whole period of the Battle (8th August–31st October, 1940) 2,375 enemy aircraft were destroyed in daylight by British fighters and anti-aircraft fire; the RAF lost 733 aircraft and 375 pilots killed.

After beating the Luftwaffe in the Battle of Britain, Fighter Command moved into the offensive. British fighters swept over the Low Countries and France and defeated the Germans over their own airfields. More than four out of every five enemy aircraft destroyed by British-based fighters in 1943 were shot down on the enemy's side of the English Channel.

Two German aircraft were destroyed for every British fighter lost in all operations during 1943.

The total number of sorties made by aircraft of Fighter Command in five and a half years of war was over 700,000.

During 1944, Fighter Command destroyed over 700 German aircraft, more than 500 of them at night.

Over 20,340 enemy aircraft were brought down by the Royal Air Force and Dominion and Allied squadrons serving with it, and by the United States Air Forces, or by British anti-aircraft fire, between September 1939 and 31st

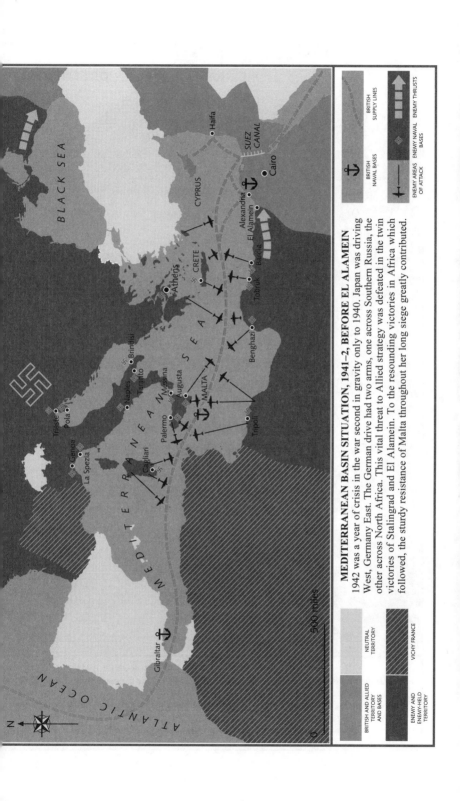

MEDITERRANEAN BASIN SITUATION, 1941–2, BEFORE EL ALAMEIN

1942 was a year of crisis in the war second in gravity only to 1940. Japan was driving West, Germany East. The German drive had two arms, one across Southern Russia, the other across North Africa. This vital threat to Allied strategy was defeated in the twin victories of Stalingrad and El Alamein. To the resounding victories in Africa which followed, the sturdy resistance of Malta throughout her long siege greatly contributed.

BRITISH AND ALLIED
TERRITORY AND BASES

NEUTRAL
TERRITORY

ENEMY AND
ENEMY-HELD
TERRITORY

VICHY FRANCE

BRITISH NAVAL BASES

BRITISH
SUPPLY LINES

ENEMY NAVAL
BASES

ENEMY THRUSTS

ENEMY AREAS
OF ATTACK

500 miles

ATLANTIC OCEAN

BLACK SEA

MEDITERRANEAN SEA

Gibraltar

La Spezia

Genoa

Trieste

Pola

Naples

Taranto

Brindisi

Messina

Palermo

Augusta

Cagliari

MALTA

Tripoli

Benghazi

Tobruk

Bardia

El Alamein

Alexandria

CRETE

Athens

CYPRUS

Haifa

SUEZ CANAL

Cairo

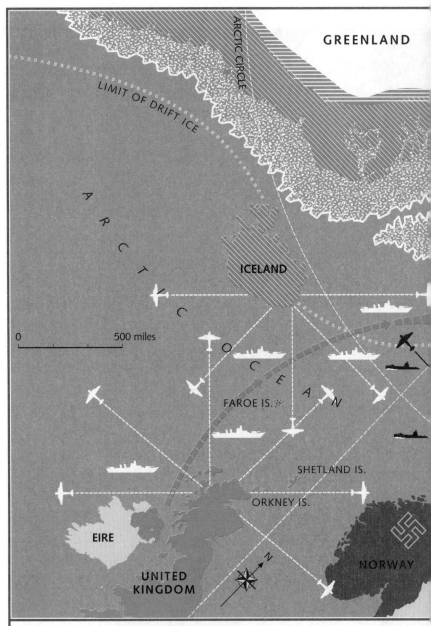

CONVOYS TO RUSSIA, THE ARCTIC ROUTE, 1942

The pledge of unstinted aid to Russia was given immediately the German assault became known.
cutting to the bare minimum supplies to the armed forces and for civilian use the goods were fou
they were pressed through the narrow and dangerous channels between the ice and the cliffs
Norway, in waters infested by the enemy's surface and underwater craft and constantly watched by
aircraft. But these convoys helped to save Russia and to add power to her return blows at the Re

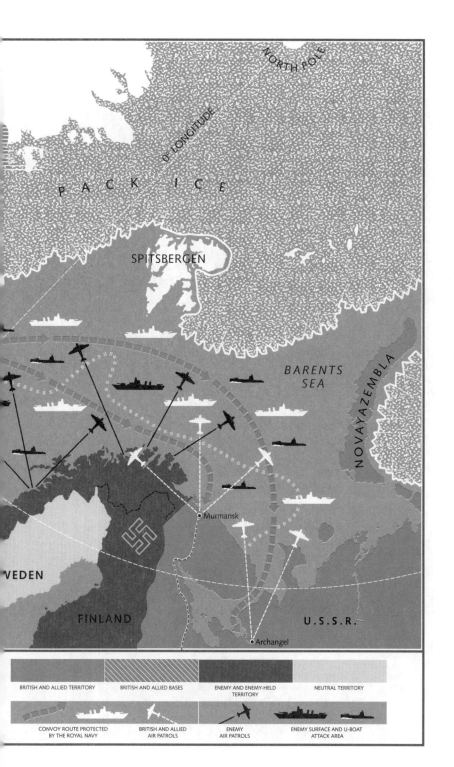

NORTH POLE

0° LONGITUDE

P A C K   I C E

SPITSBERGEN

BARENTS
SEA

NOVAYAZEMBLA

Murmansk

VEDEN

FINLAND

U.S.S.R.

Archangel

BRITISH AND ALLIED TERRITORY	BRITISH AND ALLIED BASES	ENEMY AND ENEMY-HELD TERRITORY	NEUTRAL TERRITORY

CONVOY ROUTE PROTECTED BY THE ROYAL NAVY	BRITISH AND ALLIED AIR PATROLS	ENEMY AIR PATROLS	ENEMY SURFACE AND U-BOAT ATTACK AREA

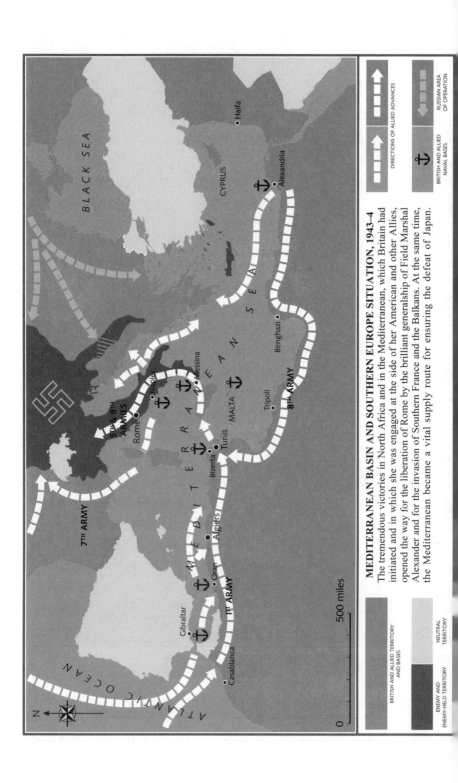

MEDITERRANEAN BASIN AND SOUTHERN EUROPE SITUATION, 1943–4

The tremendous victories in North Africa and in the Mediterranean, which Britain had initiated and in which she was engaged at the side of her American and other Allies, opened the way for the liberation of Rome by the brilliant generalship of Field Marshal Alexander and for the invasion of Southern France and the Balkans. At the same time, the Mediterranean became a vital supply route for ensuring the defeat of Japan.

BRITISH AND ALLIED TERRITORY AND BASES

ENEMY AND ENEMY-HELD TERRITORY

NEUTRAL TERRITORY

DIRECTIONS OF ALLIED ADVANCES

BRITISH AND ALLIED NAVAL BASES

RUSSIAN AREA OF OPERATION

0   500 miles

ATLANTIC OCEAN

BLACK SEA

MEDITERRANEAN SEA

Casablanca
Gibraltar
Oran
Algiers
1ST ARMY
7TH ARMY
Bizerta
Tunis
Rome
5TH & 8TH ARMIES
Naples
Messina
MALTA
Tripoli
Benghazi
8TH ARMY
CYPRUS
Haifa
Alexandria

May, 1944, over the United Kingdom, continental Europe, the Mediterranean, the Middle East, India and Burma. This figure includes at least 1,086 aircraft brought down by naval and merchant vessels or by the Fleet Air Arm, but does not include more than 6,500 destroyed by the 8th and 9th USAAFs based on Britain, nor the large numbers destroyed on the ground – well over 3,000 in the Mediterranean area alone. Axis losses in North-West Europe for the first seventy days after 6th June are given on page 69.

Fighter operations in connection with the campaign in North-West Europe are outlined elsewhere (see page 68).

In 1944 fighter aircraft operating under the Air Defence of Great Britain, and balloons, played an outstanding part in the defeat of the flying-bomb attacks on London and Southern England.

In approximately eighty days up to the end of August 1944, the enemy launched some 8,000 flying bombs against this country. Of these, 2,300 or 29 per cent got through to the London region; 25 per cent were erratic, and 46 per cent were brought down by the defences. These consisted of an arrangement of balloon, gun and fighter belts.

The guns, numbering 800 heavy and nearly 2,000 light guns and 20 American batteries, brought down 1,560 bombs. Balloons, numbering nearly 2,000, brought down 279 – nearly 15 per cent of all the bombs which entered the barrage area. Fighters brought down a further 1,900; after about a month's experience they were destroying at least 80 per cent of their sightings. The best day for the defences was 28th August when, out of 101 bombs which approached the coast, 97 were brought down.

(b) Coastal Operations

*'I cannot speak too highly of the skill, the courage and
the endurance which the crews of Coastal Command
have shown in succouring convoys and developing
offensive operations against the U-boats. The past
twelve months [1943–4] have witnessed not only a
global expansion of the Command, but also an increase
in the proportion of very-long-range aircraft which are
able to provide cover for convoys hundreds of miles out
to sea and even right across the North Atlantic.'*

RT HON. A. V. ALEXANDER, FIRST LORD OF THE ADMIRALTY,
7th March, 1944

By December 1942, Coastal Command already had more
aircraft than the entire RAF possessed at the outbreak of war.

Aircraft of Coastal Command from the outbreak of
war to May 1945 had flown well over 180,000,000 miles and
1,350,000 hours.

Over 30,000,000 miles were flown in 1943 alone, of
which 25,000,000 were flown on anti-U-boat operations.

In 1943, Coastal Command destroyed more U-boats
than in three previous years' operations put together. By
February 1944, more than 900 attacks on U-boats had been
made by Coastal Command aircraft.

Over 5,300 convoys, excluding naval convoys and
single ships, were escorted by Coastal Command during the
first three and a half years of war. This entailed more than
31,000 operational sorties.

During 1944, aircraft of Coastal Command sank
some 40 merchant ships, 3 destroyers and at least 40 other
vessels; 50 more merchant ships, 3 destroyers and a great
number of other vessels were damaged. The number of

merchant vessels sunk and damaged is almost double that of the previous year.

During June 1944, aircraft of Coastal Command flew nearly 8,000 sorties – treble the number flown in June 1943. Over 600 vessels of all types were attacked. From D-Day to the end of the year, over 8,000 anti-shipping sorties were flown by aircraft of the Command.

In the three months July to September 1944, Coastal Command put in well over 87,000 flying hours on anti-U-boat operations alone.

At least 80 per cent of the advance information required in planning the Allied landings in Normandy was provided by the aircraft of the Photographic Reconnaissance Group of Coastal Command.

(c) Bombing Operations

'It is an unfailing source of strength to us and, I well know, to our brothers-in-arms of the 8th US Bomber Command, to realize, as we do, that every bomb which leaves the racks makes smoother the part of the armies of the United Nations as they close in to the kill.'

AIR CHIEF MARSHAL SIR ARTHUR HARRIS, AOC, RAF, BOMBER COMMAND

During 1944, RAF Bomber Command dropped more than 525,000 tons of bombs. This is more than twice the weight dropped in the first four and a quarter years of war, up to December 1943. More aircraft were despatched on operational flights than in all the previous years of the war put together, yet the casualty rate was well under half of what it was in 1943. The total weight of bombs dropped by Bomber Command on Europe, from the outbreak of war to 5th May,

1945, was 955,040 tons. The total number of sorties was 392,137.

The whole operational strength of the long-range bomber force of the Luftwaffe is now only a quarter of what it was in June 1940; RAF Bomber Command, on the other hand, can now drop nearly twenty times the tonnage which it was capable of dropping in June 1940.

The greatest weight of bombs dropped in one night of 1944 was just under 5,500 tons; the greatest weight dropped in twenty-four hours was 10,300 tons. In one period of eighteen hours in October 1944, Bomber Command despatched over 2,600 aircraft.

Britain's heaviest bomb in 1944 weighed 5½ tons, approximately twenty-four times heavier than the heaviest bomb used in March 1940. It was then by far the heaviest and most powerful bomb in the world; it makes a crater 100 ft across and will penetrate at least 12 ft of concrete. In March 1945 the use of a 10-ton bomb was announced.

In twenty-four hours, Bomber Command aircraft have dropped more than twice the tonnage of explosives that the Germans dropped on Britain in four and a half months of flying-bomb attacks, and half as much again as the weight of bombs dropped on London in the ten months of the 'Blitz'.

Bomber Command fought three great battles over Germany in 1943, and took part in two great Allied campaigns in 1944: these were the battles of the Ruhr, of Hamburg and of Berlin; the pre-invasion smashing of the enemy's communications system in North-West Europe; and the Anglo-American air offensive against the enemy's fuel supplies.

The battle of the Ruhr began with a heavy attack on Essen on 5th–6th March, 1943; six months later, 50,000 tons of bombs had fallen on this vital industrial area. The battle included the breaching of the Möhne and Eder dams on 17th May, which released 336,000,000 tons of water and caused floods extending for 50 miles.

Some 10,000 tons of bombs were dropped on Hamburg by RAF and USAAF bombers between 24th July and 3rd August, 1943, and three-quarters of the city was devastated.

The battle of Berlin began on the night of 18th November, 1943, and by the end of March 1944, Berlin was the most heavily bombed city in the world, well over 33,000 tons of bombs having been dropped upon it by the RAF alone.

In April 1944, the Allied Air Forces began their great assault on the enemy's communication system in North-West Europe; RAF Bomber Command contributed 20,000 tons of bombs to this campaign.

In June 1944, Bomber Command took up its part in the joint Anglo-American oil offensive, concentrating on the ten synthetic oil plants in the Ruhr. By September 1944 these were all out of action, and by December, despite constant repairs, were all out of action again.

In addition to strategic bombing, heavy bombers of the RAF have played an important and extremely effective tactical role, by direct intervention in the land battles in North-West Europe. Some of these operations are indicated below (see page 69).

Despite these tremendous commitments, over 10 per cent of the total effort of Bomber Command has, on an average, been engaged in mine-laying operations; 47,000 mines laid by Bomber Command probably sank over a million tons of enemy shipping. Mine-laying operations in 1944 were on a far greater scale than in any previous year of the war.

(d) Air Operations in Connection with the Campaign in North-West Europe

> *'Preparations definitely began for the battle in April, not only at the point of attack, for that would have revealed much, but necessarily and impartially all along the coast and far in the rear. Thus, when our ships crossed the Channel, unseen and unmolested, half the guns that were to have blown them out of the water were already dismantled or silent, and when the counter-attack began on land and under the sea, the tactical and coastal forces held it back while our footholds on shore and our sea lanes were being firmly established.'*

RT HON. WINSTON CHURCHILL, 2nd August 1944

In the three months April–June, which saw the preparation and launching of the invasion of Europe, 7,000 men of the RAF Home Commands alone were killed or posted missing.

Allied Expeditionary Air Force

The 2nd British Tactical Air Force, and RAF Fighter Command compose, together with the 9th USAAF, the AEAF operating under Supreme Headquarters, Allied Expeditionary Forces.

The following are some outstanding records, chiefly of the two British components.

In the month of June 1944, aircraft of the AEAF flew approximately 90,000 sorties – by far the greatest monthly aggregate ever so far recorded by a single Command in the history of air warfare. Nearly a quarter of the sorties were concerned with providing cover for the Allied beachheads in Normandy; on many days more than 1,000 aircraft patrolled the landing area. The 2nd British Tactical Air Force alone flew 34,000 sorties out of this total.

In one week, 7th–15th August, the 2nd Tactical Air Force flew 8,665 sorties, more than 5,700 of which were in direct support of the Allied armies; 10,500 rockets were launched by rocket-firing fighters during the week.

On 18th August, aircraft of the 2nd Tactical Air Force intercepted a large concentration of German armour and transport attempting to escape encirclement in the Falaise pocket, and took record toll of it, accounting for more than 2,800 vehicles and 200 tanks destroyed or damaged – equal to the combined results of the eight previous best days.

The total destruction caused by AEAF fighter-bombers and fighters to the German army during August 1944 amounted to: 873 tanks, 12,441 motor transport vehicles, 1,413 locomotives, 5,926 railway wagons, and 406 river barges.

In the first seventy days of operations in France, 2,990 enemy aircraft were destroyed in the air and 651 on the ground; Allied aircraft losses of all types totalled 2,959.

During the first five days of the airborne landings in Holland RAF fighters flew more than 1,400 sorties, about 1,250 of which were in direct support of the ground forces.

From D-Day to the end of 1944, one group of the 2nd Tactical Air Force destroyed more than 200 enemy aircraft at night over the Western Front.

In all, aircraft of the 2nd Tactical Air Force fired over 150,000 rockets, dropped some 62,000 tons of bombs on German ground forces and communications, and flew approximately 300,000 sorties in close support of the Allied armies, from June 1944 to 8th May, 1945.

RAF Bomber Command

During the night of 5th–6th June, 1944, 1,300 aircraft of Bomber Command dropped well over 5,000 tons of bombs on ten coastal batteries in the Normandy landing area.

In the month of June 1944, well over 56,000 tons of bombs were dropped by the RAF; over fifty attacks were made on key railway and road points, and twenty-one coastal batteries were bombed.

The following are two outstanding examples of the close tactical support given by Bomber Command to Allied ground forces on many occasions during the fighting in North-West Europe: on the morning of 18th July more than 1,000 heavy bombers dropped 5,000 tons of bombs on enemy positions east of Caen in less than forty-five minutes, as a prelude to an advance by infantry. On the night of 7th–8th August, a similar force dropped 3,500 tons of bombs on enemy positions astride the Caen–Falaise road; this was the first time heavy bombers had operated in close support at night, yet the support was even closer than in previous daylight operations.

Between 1st–12th September, Bomber Command flew 2,042 sorties against Havre, and dropped 9,500 tons – 5,000 in one daylight raid alone. The saving of manpower thus effected was shown by the army casualties – 400 – for the taking of the port, with 11,000 prisoners.

With the advent of the war to German soil the massive blows of Bomber Command against the strategic industrial and communications centres of the Reich frequently also served important tactical ends. For instance, on 16th November, 1944, over 1,150 heavy bombers of RAF Bomber Command, escorted by more than 250 fighters, were despatched to attack Düren, Julich and Heinsberg, three fortified towns east and north-east of Aachen, in direct support of American troops; over 5,600 tons of bombs were dropped in one of the greatest air operations of the war, and photographs showed a concentration of bomb craters almost without parallel in any previous attack by the RAF.

(e) Air Operations in Connection with Mediterranean and Burma Campaigns

These campaigns were also remarkable for the coordination of air operations with those on land and on sea. Air operations, both tactical and strategic, contributed materially to the success of the campaigns in North Africa, Sicily, Italy, the Balkans and Burma. A few figures selected out of many statistics available illustrate this.

Over 20,000,000 lb of bombs were dropped on enemy objectives in North Africa between 8th November, 1942, and 7th May, 1943. On one day alone (6th May) more than 2,500 sorties were flown and 1,250,000 lb of bombs dropped. More than 7,600 Axis aircraft were destroyed in all the campaigns in North Africa – 5,156 of these in combat and 2,500 destroyed or captured on the ground.

The Allied advance up the Italian peninsula was well supported throughout by the Mediterranean Allied Air Forces. To quote only one example, the German armies retreating north from Rome were constantly harried by the Desert Air Force; in less than a month about 10,000 motor vehicles were wrecked on the roads.

In all during 1944, RAF and Dominion aircraft of the Mediterranean Allied and Middle East Air Forces flew some 218,000 sorties.

In August 1944, the RAF Balkan Air Force was created to support Marshal Tito's and other operations in the Balkans, and to organize the evacuation by air of sick and wounded partisans. From Yugoslavia alone, over 1,300 were evacuated during the months June–November.

The rapidity of the German ejection from Greece and their flight through the Balkans were largely due to the support given by RAF Spitfires and transport aircraft.

In this connection may also be mentioned the highly successful mining of the Danube carried out by RAF

Wellingtons and Liberators from Italy. This seriously restricted German supply traffic on this great inland waterway, at a time when the position of German troops in the Balkans was becoming increasingly precarious.

The achievement of air superiority enabled the 14th Army and Allied Forces to develop a new form of jungle warfare based on air transport and the dropping of supplies from the air. The transport and maintenance of the Long Range Penetration Brigades ('The Chindits') was one striking example of this. The maintenance by air of the garrisons in Manipur, the reinforcement by air of the garrisons at Imphal and Dimapur with 2½ divisions and the evacuation of 30,000 non-combatant units from these areas provided further evidence of the contribution made by the air forces to the success of the campaign.

From May to October 1944, inclusive, right through the monsoon, Allied aircraft of the Combat Cargo Task Force of Eastern Air Command flew 25,049 sorties and delivered 76,169 tons of supplies.

(f) Transport Command

Transport Command at the beginning of 1945 was flying nearly 6 million track miles a month over its worldwide network of 80,000 miles of scheduled air routes. Its aircraft were covering more than a million miles a month over the North and South Atlantic alone.

During 1944 transport aircraft of the Command's Mediterranean Group alone achieved a total of 25,000,000 ton miles, carrying a total of 247,000 passengers. In addition thousands of aircraft were handled by ferry pilots on their way to war fronts in Italy and Burma.

In little over five months since D-Day, one group of RAF Transport Command flew more than 20,000,000 lb of supplies to forward airfields on the Continent and transported 14,000 service personnel across the Channel; more than 5,000 airborne troops were dropped or landed by gliders behind the enemy lines. In addition, 4,000 panniers containing urgent supplies were dropped to troops on the ground, and hundreds of jeeps, motorcycles, anti-tank guns and other war materials.

One Transport Command airfield in Belgium has, in one month, received 3,438 aircraft, handled more than 7,000 tons of freight, received and despatched 4,280 passengers, and evacuated 7,200 casualties.

In one week, an Air Supply Group of RAF Transport Command flew more than 1,800,000 lb of freight and 48,000 lb of mail for the troops to the Western Front; more than 66,000 lb of mail and 1,290 casualties were brought home in the same period.

From D-Day to VE-Day No. 46 Group RAF Transport Command flew 13½ million miles, carried 33,000 tons of mail and freight and transported or evacuated 258,000 passengers and casualties. In twelve months, during 1944–5, the Command flew 50,000,000 air miles and 374,000,000 passenger miles.

7. THE ACHIEVEMENT OF THE CIVIL DEFENCE SERVICES

*'The courage of Londoners, and the organization of
our many defence and municipal services under
unexampled strain, not only enabled us to come through
what many might have thought a mortal peril, but
impressed itself in every country, upon the minds of
every country in the world.'*

RT HON. WINSTON CHURCHILL, 14th July, 1941

Perspective

London is fifteen minutes by air from the French coast, till lately under German occupation. That was the constant background for more than four years. The men and women of the Civil Defence services were the front-line fighters of the British people when they successfully withstood the enemy's onslaught from the air during the Battle of Britain. At the time of the Blitz 50,000 high-explosive bombs were showered down upon London between the beginning of September 1940 and the end of July 1941. The number of firebombs dropped was far larger.

These men and women have again become front-line fighters with the launching of V-bomb attacks against London and Southern England. From the middle of June 1944 up to 6th September, over 8,000 of these bombs had been launched. Rocket bombs have also been fired against Britain.

Performance

London was bombed every night except three from the 7th September to the end of November 1940. Yet life and war work within the capital were never fatally interrupted. This was due in great measure to the men and women of the Civil Defence services – wardens, firemen, police, rescue squads, drivers, nurses and auxiliaries.

There were 324,000 men and 59,000 women in the whole-time Civil Defence services in 1941. In the following year 20,000 additional women had released an equivalent number of men for national service elsewhere.

In addition there were 1¼ million men and 350,000 women giving part-time service.

Nearly 10,000 fires were attended to by the London fire brigade and their reinforcements during the first twenty-two days and nights of the blitz. More than 4,600,000 men and women civilian fire guards were organized in 1941 to counter the enemy's fire-raising tactics.

3,000 incendiary bombs were dropped and twenty fires were started in one very sharp raid on a town on the south-west coast. Fire guards dealt with these so effectively that the National Fire Service had to be called out only to two of these fires.

Some 31,000 instructors have been trained in special schools for Civil Defence. More than 40,000 instructors have been engaged in training fire guards.

The system of water supply was so efficiently maintained during the Blitz that no cases of typhoid occurred. Hygiene was so well maintained that despite the crowding of London's air-raid shelters there was no increase in disease.

Between September 1940 and September 1941, Post Office engineers repaired, in the London Region alone, 1,700 cables, 3,000 joints, and 500,000 wires.

During the Blitz the Post Office was still handling 10,000,000 packets and 500,000 parcels daily.

Out of 13,000,000 houses in the United Kingdom, 4½ million had been damaged or destroyed by bombs from the start of war up to September 1944. That is nearly one out of every three houses in the country. Of this total, 202,000 were totally destroyed, and a further 255,000 rendered uninhabitable.

3,500 mobile volunteers have been formed into a labour corps known as the Special Service Flying Squad. This squad, housed and fed in travelling caravans, supplements local resources in severe air attacks. It has dealt with more than 160,000 cases of intensive repair to bomb-damaged houses, and industrial objectives.

After one raid on towns on the east coast of Scotland flying squads of repair-workers got on the job with such effective dispatch that families who had to leave their damaged houses were back within a few hours.

Nearly 14,000 churches and other ecclesiastical buildings, 1,103 schools and about 500 hospitals had been destroyed or damaged in Great Britain, up to September 1944.

Very many of Britain's provincial cities suffered greatly in the Blitz. Plymouth, for instance, was savagely bombed by the Germans five times between 21st and 29th April, 1941. Many Civil Defence depots and posts were demolished or damaged and there were numbers of casualties among the personnel. During April, twenty-seven of the wardens alone were killed or seriously injured. But Civil Defence carried on in Plymouth, and on the last night of the April attacks 12,000 citizens were organized and brigaded as firebomb fighters, apart from the unorganised volunteers. Other cities severely damaged during 1940–1 were Bristol, Cardiff, Birmingham, Sheffield, Manchester, Liverpool, Glasgow, Nottingham, Leeds, etc.

Since November 1942, there have been numbers of sharp raids on British towns, including London, Canterbury, Aberdeen, Great Yarmouth, Sunderland, Cardiff, Brighton, Bournemouth, Torquay, Grimsby, Hull.

At the time of the great Blitz on Coventry roughly 80,000 people were working in that district. It took only fourteen days to get 77,000 of them back to work.

After eight nights of Blitz on the docks at Liverpool, every shift was working in about three days after the attack had ceased.

Up to the end of 1943, 2,889 decorations and commendations for bravery had been made to members of the Civil Defence services in Britain.

One warden in every six during the Battle of Britain was a woman. The women of Britain know about war. So do many of the children, because when war came to Britain it was total.

In all, between June 1944 and March 1945, over 9,000 flying bombs were launched against Britain. In addition, 1,050 rockets fell between September 1944 and March 1945.

During the first three and a half months of the flying-bomb attacks, about 25,000 houses were totally destroyed and over 1,000,000 received damage. In one period of eighty days, damage was done to 140 schools, 103 churches, 98 hospitals and 112 public-houses.

When the flying bombs arrived, only 21,000 men were at work on repairs in London. Now there are 132,000; of these, 44,900 have been brought in from the provinces. In London alone 258,849 houses had been repaired by 19th December, 1944, and 719,300 were scheduled for repair during winter.

Under the official evacuation scheme, reintroduced since the start of the flying-bomb attacks, more than 755,000 mothers and children were evacuated from London and Southern England.

Civil Defence Rescue workers have received constant and intensive training in scientific methods of rescue, with the result that the average time taken to extricate a victim from a wrecked building has been reduced by more than half, compared with the days of the 'Blitz'. A quite considerable number of members of the National Fire Service have also received this training. Some British troops, Home Guards, US troops and members of other Allied forces have been given the rudiments of the training.

Whole-time workers of the National Fire Service have also made an important contribution to the war effort when they are not actually firefighting and training. They do work on fire stations, static water apparatus, public lighting, etc. In rural areas they help in harvesting, and in towns they have done a great deal of productive work on camouflage-netting, parts for sten-guns, etc.

8. THE ACHIEVEMENT OF BRITISH ECONOMIC WARFARE

Perspective

The object of all economic warfare – acting continuously in one form or another – is to limit and, if possible, break the economic power of the enemy to keep fighting. Thus it forms an important part of the total war effort. Britain has, accordingly, since 3rd September, 1939, carried on coordinated economic warfare against the whole process of Germany's productive capacity – supplies of materials, output of arms and machines, transport facilities, general organization, manpower and stamina. This warfare is conducted by two chief means: first, the limitation through naval blockade of the flow of goods and raw materials to the enemy, combined with special commercial and financial measures in neutral countries; and second, the direct destruction of enemy supplies, transport, and means of production by aerial bombing. The British blockade cuts off German-dominated Europe from vital sources of supply overseas, especially the rich areas of the Far East temporarily controlled by the Japanese. The financial and commercial measures include: restriction of imports from overseas to neutral countries in Europe to fit their domestic requirements only, so that there should be no surplus which might find its way into German hands; in so far as these countries have domestic surpluses which the enemy needs, the taking of steps to buy them up (pre-emptive purchase); and the blacklisting of enemy firms so as to limit the scope of their activities. The blockade leads to tightening-up of the enemy's economy, creating strains and reducing its flexibility.

This increases the effectiveness of the direct bombing attacks at selected key points in German industry (e.g. synthetic oil) and transport. Both the blockade and air attack have done much to accentuate Germany's main weakness – shortage of manpower.

All the Allies are participating in economic warfare, but Britain's contribution has been unique. From the very first day of the war the blockade has been in action, causing an unspectacular, but continuous and cumulative strain on enemy resources. It had already been applied for over two years before America entered the war. Since the beginning of 1942, the USA has been adding an ever-increasing weight, particularly in the air attacks on the enemy which had reached new high peaks of intensity in 1944. Similarly, the Russians – since the middle of 1941 – have not only forced the Germans to sacrifice vast numbers of men and enormous supplies, but have also prevented them from obtaining in the USSR the means of countering the effects of the blockade and air attack in the West. The citizens of enemy-occupied territories, too, have played their part by carrying out sabotage and adopting 'go slow' methods of war. But underlying all these efforts of her Allies lies Britain's achievements – consistent since September 1939 – upon which the economic warfare of the other United Nations could be based and coordinated with her own in a concerted effort.

Performance

(a) Blockade

> *'Nearly all the German ocean-going ships are in hiding and rusting in neutral harbours, while our world-wide trade steadily proceeds.'*

> RT HON. WINSTON CHURCHILL, 12th November, 1939

The blockade has virtually cut Germany off from all non-European sources of oil imports, all her natural rubber, about three-quarters of her copper, practically all her cotton and over two-thirds of her wool requirements.

The constant factor of the blockade forced Germany to rely on limited sources of ferro-alloys (chrome, nickel, manganese, tungsten and molybdenum) – used for toughening steel – and has thus accentuated the importance of recent developments affecting their supply, i.e. the loss of Nikopol, the bombing of Knaben, and the loss of Turkish and Spanish imports. About 80 per cent of Germany's nickel supplies were cut off by the blockade and proportionately greater use had to be made of manganese and molybdenum in certain alloys. The supply position of molybdenum has, however, constituted a major problem since the only European source of any significance is Norway, and the bombing of the Knaben mines (putting them out of action for several months), which accounted for over three-quarters of Germany's current supplies, has seriously impaired the situation. There are no important tungsten deposits in German-occupied Europe and supplies from the Iberian peninsula, which left no margin for reserve stocks, were greatly reduced in June 1944 when Portugal agreed to prohibit further exports, and supplies from Spain were also reduced.

The effect of the blockade on the oil position has been twofold. First, it had undoubtedly handicapped operations at the fronts, and second, compelled the Germans to depend more on synthetic production, with the consequent diversion of labour and materials. Shortage of lubricating oils has contributed to deterioration of rolling stock and affected industrial production.

The sealing off of all supplies of natural rubber has meant a great expansion in synthetic rubber production, but, quite apart from the fact that this is more expensive in labour

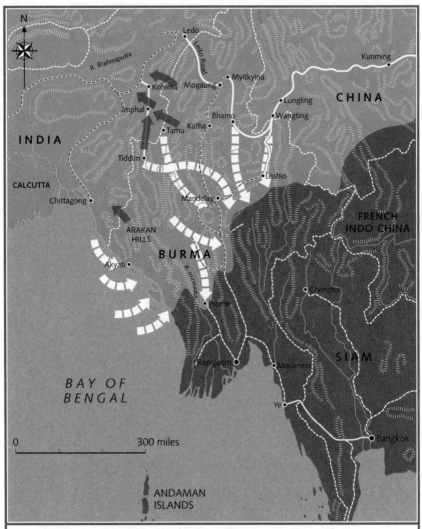

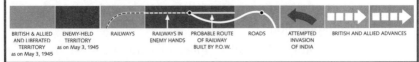

THE BURMA FRONT

The invasion of Burma completed for Japan the blockade of China and gave her a base for her intended invasion of India. Burma became the principal land front for the Western Allies against Japan. The British 14th Army, which numbered 750,000 during 1944, fighting in appalling conditions of climate and vegetation, had nevertheless by the end of the year finally removed the threat to India, and in 1945 broke the Japanese blockade of China. Throughout 1943 and 1944 the Burma campaign was putting an almost intolerable strain on Japanese shipping and thus largely contributing to Allied victories in the Pacific.

| BRITISH & ALLIED AND LIBERATED TERRITORY as on May 3, 1945 | ENEMY-HELD TERRITORY as on May 3, 1945 | RAILWAYS | RAILWAYS IN ENEMY HANDS | PROBABLE ROUTE OF RAILWAY BUILT BY P.O.W. | ROADS | ATTEMPTED INVASION OF INDIA | BRITISH AND ALLIED ADVANCES |

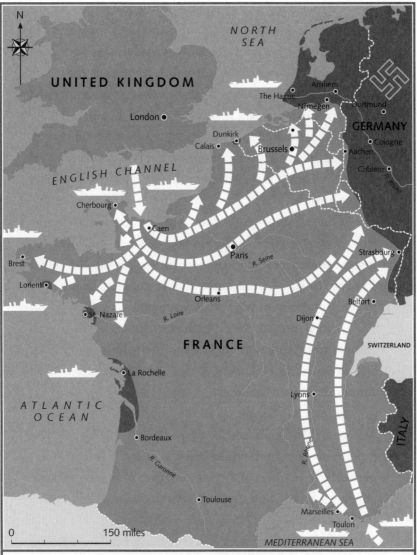

THE WESTERN FRONT, 15ᵗʰ DECEMBER, 1944

From the first day of the war Britain had prepared herself as an offensive base against Germany and had endured endless discomforts and much bloody suffering to maintain the integrity of the base. After months of devastating air attack against the enemy, the reward came in June 1944, when she saw her own forces and those of her Allies launched at great hazard, but with complete success, against the formidable defences of the Nazis' Fortress of Europe.

| BRITISH AND LIBERATED TERRITORY | ENEMY AND ENEMY-HELD TERRITORY | NEUTRAL TERRITORY | MAIN AREA OF NAVAL ACTIVITY | BRITISH AND ALLIED ADVANCES |

and materials than the production of goods to pay for the import of the natural product, in many cases the quality of the substitute is inferior. Recently, the Germans have been forced to manufacture tyres for military purposes entirely of buna, although this means a great decline in durability and an increase in wastage.

It is estimated that the production of all substitutes including buna use up about one-quarter of Germany's total electricity output as well as a considerable proportion of her labour force.

The interception of enemy blockade-runners by the Royal Navy resulted in the sinking of seven out of eleven inward-bound blockade-runners in the period November 1942 to April 1943, and in the almost complete failure from the enemy's point of view of later attempts.

British pre-emptive purchases denied Germany all chrome from Turkey from 1940 to the early part of 1943, and in April 1944 Turkey agreed to the cessation of all chrome exports to the Reich.

Britain has bought up all the surplus woollen goods in Turkey and in Spain. The consequences of this action were experienced by the German armies on the Russian Front, particularly in the winter campaigns. In all pre-emptive purchases Britain and the United States have acted in complete cooperation.

The British Statutory List (the Black List) has successfully immobilized enemy firms in countries overseas. Germany and her agents have been prevented from availing themselves of the foreign assets of their satellites and the enemy-occupied countries by effective freezing measures.

The principal effect of the blockade on agricultural policy has been a greater concentration on such crops as oilseeds (to make up for the shortage of fats) and roots – crops which require considerable care and have probably used up more valuable labour. It is estimated that the numbers employed in German agriculture have increased by one million on the pre-war figure, as a result of the impossibility of obtaining overseas supplies.

Over 95 per cent of the pre-war requirements of natural phosphates were imported, and allocations of phosphoric fertilisers even before the North African campaign were only one-third of normal consumption. Since then, Germany has been dependent upon basic slag as a source of phosphoric acid. In July 1944, it was announced that only 18 per cent of the peacetime consumption of phosphate fertilisers would be allowed to farmers for the year 1944–5. On 30th November the ration was reduced to as little as 6 per cent of pre-war consumption – no doubt a consequence of the cutting off of Lorraine iron ores from the smelting of which Germany had been obtaining her basic slag.

The Royal Navy has successfully prevented sea traffic between Germany and Italy, and Germany and the Balkans. This has forced the enemy to make greater use of railways and inland waterways, instead of sea transport.

Negotiations by the Allies with the Swedish Government secured (on 18th August, 1944) the withdrawal of marine insurance for all Swedish ships sailing to any Axis port whatsoever, thus in effect imposing a complete embargo on their shipowners. Moreover, on 27th September, the Swedish Government closed all their own Baltic ports to German shipping.

The effect of the Swedish Government's action is to deprive the Germans of the bulk of their remaining imports from Sweden, the most important of which is iron ore, of which 60–65 per cent has been carried in Swedish ships. Some shipments may of course still leave Narvik, but the total quantity of ore to have reached Germany in 1944 was about one-third less than the quantity contracted for under the trade agreement, and less than 50 per cent of what the Germans actually received during the whole of 1943. The cutting of the Dortmund–Ems canal contributed to the reduction in iron ore reaching the Ruhr.

During the course of 1944 representatives of Great Britain and the United States reached an agreement with the Swedish concern, SKF, whereby exports of ball-bearings to Germany were substantially reduced. On 15th October it was announced by the Swedish Foreign Office that these exports had been entirely stopped.

Another result of negotiation has been the Swedish decision to end the export to the Axis of machine tools, special tools and chemicals.

British control of the English Channel by mine-laying and patrolling has prevented practically all enemy commercial traffic passing through the Straits of Dover.

In short, the continuous blockade has compelled the Germans to use large quantities of materials and labour in the production of substitutes for normally imported goods and in the policy of increased self-sufficiency in foodstuffs, and has thus reduced the supply of labour available for other war production. The blockade is a long-term operation which has paved the way for the present disintegration of the German economy.

(b) Bombing Operations

'We know, not merely what factory has been hit, but which shop in the factory, and what is was producing... we can read some at least of the reasons why Germany has no longer abundant manpower and materials to throw into the offensive; repair and defence must have first claim.'

RT HON. SIR ARCHIBALD SINCLAIR, 29th February, 1944

It is estimated that, as a result of Bomber Command's ninety-six major attacks on twenty-nine industrial towns in Germany between 1st March and 31st December, 1943, the German war industry suffered a loss of some 2,400,000,000 man-hours. The towns selected manufactured more than half the electrical engineering products, machine tools and rubber products, and nearly half the aero-engines made in the whole of Greater Germany. The loss of man-hours inflicted by Bomber Command represents 30 per cent of their potential output during the whole year.

Nearly two-thirds of Krupp's armaments works at Essen was damaged in attacks between March and July 1943, resulting in a loss of at least six months' production; some 10 million square feet of floor space were affected.

In the spring of 1944 it was estimated that production in Berlin, the enemy's largest single manufacturing centre, was at least 40 per cent below what it was in the previous year.

By the end of 1944, thirteen major German industrial centres had each received 10,000 tons of bombs, and the total area of industrial devastation in Germany had reached at least 36,000 acres.

The bombing of Germany's heavy industrial concentrations by the RAF had another effect complementary, in particular, to the attacks of the 8th USAAF on the German aircraft industry. It deprived the enemy of the means of rebuilding his destroyed fighter factories, and caused profound dislocation throughout the whole structure of the industry.

Another important objective of the Anglo-American bombing offensive was the German ball-bearings industry, with its vital relationship to every category of war production. As a result mainly of bombing, it was estimated in March 1944 that the output of ball-bearings was only 50 per cent of that of the previous summer.

Another form taken by the Allied air attacks against the German war economy, is that against the German transport system. A tremendous weight of bombs has been and is being dropped on German railway centres, seriously reducing their overall traffic capacity, destroying rolling stock and locomotives, and with them, their repair facilities. The destruction of rail installations is particularly serious for Germany, as she has lost, in Nikopol, her main source of manganese, of which a high proportion is required in the manufacture of points.

As well as inflicting heavy losses on what may be described as Germany's railway capital, the bombing of the German transport system results in the slow paralysis of her industrial machinery. This in its turn must seriously impede such projects as the movement of factories underground to escape from bombing.

At the same time, the enemy is being denied the possibility of making good his losses in railway capacity by the use of inland waterways. The mining of the Kiel Canal shortly before D-Day resulted in its being closed for over a week, and it was estimated that 1,350,000 metric tons of cargo were held up at a very critical time. The embankments of both the Dortmund–Ems and Mitteland Canals have also been cut by bombing, and stretches of 16 and 15 miles respectively of the canals drained. This meant that inland waterway communications between the Ruhr and the Rhine on one hand, and North, Central and Eastern Europe on the other, were effectively cut for some time.

In April 1944, the Anglo-American Air Forces opened what has been described as the first major air attack, with adequate resources, upon the economic vitals of an enemy power. This was the attack on Germany's oil supplies – or more specifically, upon the refineries and synthetic oil production plants under German control.

About one-third of German Europe's total oil require-ments were met by the refineries of the great Rumanian oilfield at Ploesti. When the Russians entered Ploesti in August 1944, it was found that the output of Rumanian oil had been reduced to less than a third of what it had been four months previously, as a result of bombing.

Rather more than another third of Germany's oil sup-plies come from her synthetic oil plants, and the rest from new oilfields in Germany, Austria and Hungary. By constant bombing of these plants and refineries, it was estimated in September that production was less than 25 per cent of capacity before the offensive was launched. By March 1945 synthetic oil output had dropped to 10 per cent.

The German reaction to this offensive is significant. Overriding priority has been given to the repair of the affected plants, and permanent repair camps have been built alongside the major synthetic oil plants. Hardly a drop of oil is being used in German war industry; all industrial vehicles run on producer gas. There is evidence that military opera-tions, both on the ground and in the air, are definitely being handicapped for lack of fuel.

9. THE ACHIEVEMENT OF BRITAIN'S AID TO HER ALLIES

Perspective

This war is being fought on the principle of mutual aid and the pooling of resources. Generous American lend-lease became translated into mutual aid when the United States entered the war. This was confirmed by Britain's mutual aid agreement with the United States in February 1942. It was estimated in November 1943 that mutual aid expenditure by Britain currently amounted to 10 per cent of Britain's war expenditure. The nature of Britain's reciprocal aid makes it impossible to give complete money values.

Nor does mutual aid cover the whole of overseas expenditure. Pay of troops and expenditures in third countries are outside its scope. Britain has borne a particularly heavy share of this burden. Up to the end of June 1944, the United Kingdom had sold overseas assets to the value of £1,065 million and incurred liabilities abroad amounting to over £2,300 million.

The total of Britain's mutual aid, as recorded, exceeds £1,000 million. This has been given in furtherance of the principle that the resources of the United Nations should be pooled for the common war effort.

Performance

(a) To the United States

> *'These two great organizations of the English-speaking democracies, the British Empire and the United States,*

> *will have to be somewhat mixed up together in some of*
> *their affairs for mutual and general advantage.'*

RT HON. WINSTON CHURCHILL, 20th August, 1940

Britain has, not withstanding the lend-lease arrangement, spent over £1,500 million in the United States on supplies of all kinds since the outbreak of war.

In September 1940, Britain leased to the United States for ninety-nine years without charge naval and air bases on British island possessions in the Western Atlantic; this in return for the most timely gift of fifty over-age American destroyers.

About 56 million square feet of covered storage, workshop space, hangars and general accommodation has been provided for the US War Department, together with petrol and munition depots, garages; and some 33 million square feet of open storage for the US Army. Hospitals to the extent of nearly 100,000 beds have been specially built, or turned over, and all stores such as furniture, bedding, crockery and cooking utensils have been provided and maintained for the whole of the accommodation handed over.

By the end of June 1944, 133 airfields, with their depots, headquarters and ancillary accommodation, had been provided for the USAAF.

Excluding construction materials and petrol, US forces in the United Kingdom received almost 6,800,000 ships' tons of supplies and equipment in the two years ended 30th June, 1944. Over half of this was provided in the last six months of that period.

31 per cent of all supplies and equipment currently required by the US Army in the European theatre of operations between 1st June, 1942, and 30th June, 1944, was supplied as reciprocal aid.

Sparking plugs for certain US aircraft have been wholly

provided from United Kingdom production. Altogether 558,500 had been requisitioned up to 30th June, 1944, while in addition 600,000 plugs had been shipped to the United States.

US forces in Britain have been provided with many other types of supplies, including bombs, shells, ammunition, anti-tank equipment, 2,104 aircraft (of which 500 were 'Horsa' gliders), with an additional 570 aero-engines, 137,000 jettison fuel tanks, 50,000 pieces of armour plate for aircraft, 29,000 aero tyres, 22,000 aero tubes. 7,087,802 jerricans (specially constructed petrol cans) were delivered during the first six months of 1944.

The equipment and tools of a complete anti-aircraft gun barrel factory, and, for example, shell-producing plants, have been sent from Britain to the United States as reciprocal aid.

Britain has sent America, free of charge, machine-tools, anti-aircraft guns, ammunition, Rolls-Royce engines and thousands of barrage balloons.

Britain has supplied America with her newest inventions such as radio-locators, astrographs, and the jet-propulsion aero-engine.

Bailey Bridges were provided to US forces as reciprocal aid, and the design was made available so that the bridge could be manufactured in the United States for use in other theatres of operations.

Rockets based on a British design are now being used by American forces against the Japanese in the Pacific.

Britain supplied the basic design for the American 'Liberty' ship.

Many thousands of charts, in addition to regular supplies of charts to Washington, have been provided to US warships and establishments concerned in invasion operations.

The items supplied as reciprocal aid range from the full use of the world's two greatest liners, the *Queen Mary* and *Queen Elizabeth*, to carry American troops across the ocean to the provision of 16 million boxes of matches for US Army post exchanges; from 14,120,000 rounds of ammunition and 587,000 smoke and other chemical warfare generators to 33,340,000 lb of nails and 11,000 telegraph poles; from 200 mobile wharf cranes and 180 miles of new railway track to 37,250,000 cakes of soap and 7,800,000 lb of salt.

Quantities of radio equipment have been provided, including the total requirements of both the US 8th and 15th Air Forces for one secret type of set, in the first six months of 1944.

Transportation of US Army stores and personnel during the six months ended 30th June, 1944, required 650,000 wagons and 9,225 special trains. Nineteen ambulance trains and sixteen mobile workshops and breakdown trains were put at the disposal of the US forces. In addition, hundreds of thousands of tons of US stores were transported by road and canal.

For the invasion operations extensive underground headquarters were constructed with an intricate system of communication for controlling shipping and small craft. In addition to the specially constructed landing craft bases, maintenance bases and embarkation facilities, items handed over to the US forces included 2 complete floating docks, 2,100 pontoon units, about 200 cranes, 12 coasters and 30 lighters, 3 hospital carriers and 2 train ferry steamers adapted for use in damaged ports. For three months the entire output of Britain's sheet steel rolling industry was devoted to the waterproofing of many hundreds of US wading tanks, as well as trucks and other mechanized equipment.

The most critical single project undertaken by the United Kingdom as reciprocal aid was the production in

Britain of virtually all the artificial harbour equipment used on the beaches of France.

Britain does not waste manpower keeping detailed accounts of each item of aid, and no monetary value could in any case be put on many items. Subject to these limitations, the estimated value of aid furnished to the US forces in Britain up to 30th June, 1944, was goods and services £343,632,000 and capital facilities £167,600,000. Food and raw materials exported to the United States by Britain up to 30th June, 1944, totalled £13,613,000 and other supplies exported to or transferred in the United States totalled £25,135,000. Aid afforded to US forces in British Colonies and in overseas theatres of war amounted to £54,750,000. Grand total of these figures is £604,730,000.

(b) To the USSR

> 'We shall give whatever help we can to Russia and the Russian people. We shall appeal to all our friends and allies in every part of the world to take the same course and pursue it, as we shall, faithfully and steadfastly to the end. We have offered the Government of Soviet Russia any technical or economic assistance which is in our power, and which is likely to be of service to them.'

RT HON. WINSTON CHURCHILL, 22nd June, 1941

Britain has furnished war material free of cost to the USSR since she became engaged in war with Germany. By September 1941, Britain had already shipped to Russia substantial quantities of rubber, tin, wool, lead, jute and shellac.

Between 1st October, 1941, and 31st March, 1944, Britain supplied to Russia 5,031 tanks, 4,020 vehicles including lorries and ambulances, 2,463 Bren carriers and 1,706 motorcycles.

Weapons and ammunition supplied up to 31st March, 1944, included 800 PIAT with 85,000 rounds of ammunition, 636 2-pdr anti-tank guns with 2,591,000 rounds of ammunition, and 3,200 Boys anti-tank rifles with 1,761,000 rounds of ammunition.

The total number of fighter aircraft despatched from Britain to Russia up to the end of March 1944 was 6,778 (including 2,672 from the United States).

Naval supplies to Russia up to 31st March, 1944, included 9 mine-sweeping trawlers, 3 motor minesweepers, and 3,006 mines.

Industrial equipment supplied to Russia up to 31st March, 1944, included machine tools to the value of £8,218,000, power plant to the value of £4,250,000, electrical equipment to the value of £3,314,000, and various types of machinery to the value of £3,019,000.

Britain opened up a route to carry supplies across Persia, as well as sending quantities of materials by the northern sea route, by which 677 cargo ships (91.6 per cent) out of a total of 739 which sailed, had arrived safely by March 1945. 75 British warships of varying sizes escorted one of the largest convoys in the early autumn of 1942. Up to June 1942, Britain provided nearly 90 per cent of the ships sailing by the northern route. In order to get the stuff to Russia by the northern route British convoys often had to beat their way through foul weather and heavy enemy attacks.

Half a million pairs of boots were shipped from Britain to Russia within one week of the German invasion of the USSR. By April 1942, the entire 3,000,000 pairs of boots asked for by Russia had been shipped from Britain at a cost of 40,000 tons of shipping-space.

In four days alone the Quartermaster-General's Department of the British Army baled, packed and despatched to Russia enough greatcoat cloth to stretch from the White Sea to the Black Sea.

In the course of the year ended 30th June, 1944, supplies shipped to the USSR included material for all three arms of the Soviet fighting forces. 1,042 tanks were sent, 6,135 miles of cable and over 2 million metres of camouflage netting. Naval supplies included 195 guns of various calibres with 4,644,930 rounds of ammunition.

The amount involved during the year to 30th June, 1944, is estimated at £90,457,000 and the total to that date at £269,457,000.

(c) To China and Other Allies

'We are determined to extend to the Chinese people
every material, moral, and spiritual help in our power.'

RT HON. WINSTON CHURCHILL, 5th July, 1942

Britain has supplied, free of charge, arms, munitions and military equipment to Chinese forces in China within the limitations of transport from India.

In addition Chinese troops, in Burma and in India, have been given all they require locally, whether by issue from British Army stocks or by local purchase, including rations and pay in local currency together with cash for local purchases, on lend-lease terms.

In November 1943, Britain had on loan to her Allies one cruiser, 14 destroyers, 17 corvettes, 6 submarines, 16 motor torpedo-boats, 17 motor launches, 19 minesweeping vessels and 4 frigates.

Credits formed most of the assistance which Britain gave to her Allies, other than the USA and the USSR, prior to her lend-lease arrangements with them. Britain's credits to her Allies, other than the USA and the USSR, together with such lend-lease assistance as Britain had provided before then, totalled about £186,000,000 by 31st December, 1942.

Up to 30th June, 1944, the estimated total of mutual aid afforded to China and other allies by Britain was £205,461,000. This consisted of: China £9,050,000, France £13,600,000 (up to 30th June, 1943, only), Poland £120,000,000 (provisional), Greece £12,368,000, Czecho-slovakia £18,629,000, Portugal £11,133,000, and Turkey £20,681,000.

The British Broadcasting Corporation has afforded to the Allied Governments in exile the opportunity of address-ing their own broadcasts from London to their own people in German-occupied Europe, by enabling them to participate in the production of the BBC programmes or by giving them periods of 'free time' for their own programmes. At the end of 1944 five European Allied Governments were receiving 'free time' in the BBC services, totalling 2¾ hours daily, and in addition some of the Allied Governments were allocated time hired by the British Government on the Cairo transmitters.

At the end of 1944 the BBC was broadcasting to conti-nental Europe a daily news service in twenty-one languages: English, French, German, Italian, Spanish, Portuguese, Norwegian, Swedish, Danish, Finnish, Albanian, Bulgarian, Czech, Dutch, Flemish, Greek, Hungarian, Polish, Ruman-ian, Serbo-Croat and Slovene. Additional transmissions in Luxembourg patois and Slovak made twenty-three languages in all.

There were 158 transmissions in every twenty-four hours in European languages including English for Europe, and many of these being simultaneous, the BBC was actually broadcasting to Europe for over forty-three hours during a twenty-four-hour day.

Up to the Allied invasion of Europe, daily half-hourly transmissions in morse brought the latest news to the editors of the hundreds of underground papers secretly published in the German-occupied countries.

At the end of 1944 the BBC was also broadcasting in Afrikaans, Arabic, Bengali, Burmese, Cantonese, Gaelic, Greek for Cyprus, Gujarati, Hindustani, Hokkien, Japanese, Kuoyu, Malay, Maltese, Marathi, Moroccan Arabic, Persian, Portuguese for Latin America, Sinhalese, Spanish for Latin America, Tamil, Thai, Turkish and Welsh, making a total of forty-seven languages in which broadcasts were being delivered.

10. THE ACHIEVEMENT OF BRITISH WAR PRODUCTION

Perspective

The immense achievements of British war production could have been made only by a great industrial nation whose workers accepted the demands of war as the first and almost the only claim upon their energies. The monthly output of munitions in the United Kingdom in the first half of 1944 was about six times as great as at the outbreak of war. This increase relates to the overall rate of production of naval and merchant vessels, aircraft, ground munitions and other munitions and warlike stores. Of the total amount of munitions produced by, or made available to, the British Commonwealth and Empire since the beginning of the war, it is estimated that about seven-tenths has been produced in the United Kingdom, while about one-tenth has come from other Empire countries. The remaining one-fifth of Empire supplies has come from the United States; of this total American contribution about one-fifth has taken the form of British cash purchases.

Performance

(a) Aircraft and Bombs

At the beginning of the war, total deliveries of new aircraft were at the rate of 730 a month, and over a quarter of these were trainers. By 1943 the average rate of deliveries had trebled, and as measured by structure-weight had increased nearly sixfold.

Output was changed to larger and more powerful types of aircraft, particularly heavy bombers. 2,889 heavy bombers were delivered in the first six months of 1944, compared with only forty-one in the whole of 1940.

The total number of aircraft produced in the United Kingdom from September 1939 to June 1944 was 102,609, divided as follows:

Heavy bombers	10,018
Medium and light bombers	17,702
Fighters	38,025
Naval	6,208
Trainers	25,346
General reconnaisance, transport, air-sea rescue and others	5,310
	102,609

More than three-quarters of the total structure-weight of aircraft delivered to the RAF and Fleet Air Arm during 1943 was provided from production in Britain.

There are as many as 70,000 different pieces and shapes of fabricated materials in a single aircraft.

Engine output increased from 1,130 a month at the end of 1939 to an average of 5,270 a month between January and June 1944. Over the same period the average horsepower of engines produced was doubled. The total number of engines produced from September 1939 to June 1944 was 208,701.

Repairs were made to 60,099 aircraft and 113,005 aero-engines from July 1940 to June 1944. For every six aircraft newly produced in 1943, four aircraft underwent major repairs in the United Kingdom.

Bomb loads increased with the size and power of the bombers produced. In 1939 the average bomb load was 1.2 tons per bomber; in 1943 it was 4.0 tons.

The weight of bombs which could be carried a distance of 1,000 miles in one sortie by the monthly output of bombers increased from 210 tons in 1,939 to more than 3,000 tons at the beginning of 1944.

The weight of filled bombs produced from the beginning of the war to June 1944 was 973,400 tons.

The bombs in general use in 1940 weighed 500 lb. In March 1942, 4,000-lb bombs were used for the first time, in September 1942, bombs weighing 8,000 lb came into use, and in March 1944, 12,000-lb bombs were being used. A year later the use of a 22,000-lb bomb was announced.

(b) Ships

From September 1939 to June 1944 the production of naval vessels in the United Kingdom was as follows :

Major naval vessels	722
Mosquito naval craft	1,386
Other naval vessels (including landing craft)	3,636

The manpower available for shipbuilding has necessarily been limited by the vital need for aircraft and army equipment after the earlier German successes, and also by the large number of men required for the refit and repair of ships continuously at sea and frequently in action.

Britain has concentrated her main effort on naval work. It was announced in March 1944 that about 70 per cent of her total effort in new construction was devoted to it.

It is now necessary to arm regular warships with many offensive and defensive weapons additional to those fitted in the early stages of the war. Much additional equipment is required in the way of radar and wireless apparatus, control gear and devices for protection against the various forms of enemy attack, including surface craft, U-boats, aircraft and mines of the magnetic and other types.

The increase in ships has called for an even greater increase in naval munitions, production of which from September 1939 to June 1944 was as follows:

Naval guns	49,865
Ammunition (excluding 20 mm)	33,335,000 rounds
Mines and depth charges	897,274
Torpedoes	17,677

The tonnage of merchant vessels constructed in the United Kingdom in the years 1940 to 1943 averaged nearly one-fifth more than in the years 1915 to 1918. Many of these vessels were of types specially designed to meet particular operational and other war needs, and were not adaptable to methods of mass construction. The gross tonnage completed from September 1939 to the end of 1943 was 4,717,000.

Practically every merchant ship must be equipped with complete defensive armament including many of the weapons and devices fitted in war vessels.

At one period the amount of merchant shipping in hand for repair was over 2½ million gross tons.

(c) Tanks and Vehicles

Output of tanks from September 1939 to June 1944 was 25,116, of carriers and armoured cars 74,802, and of wheeled vehicles for the Services 919,111.

Fighting vehicles are now heavier and more highly powered than they were at the outbreak of war.

(d) Guns, Ammunition and Other Supplies

From September 1939 to June 1944 the following ground munitions were produced:

Field, medium and heavy artillery equipments	13,512
Heavy anti-aircraft equipments	6,294

Light anti-aircraft equipments	15,324
Machine guns and sub-machine guns	3,729,921
Rifles	2,001,949
Gun ammunition	161,100,000 rounds
20-mm ammunition	387,700,000 rounds
Small arms ammunition	8,285,000,000 rounds
Grenades	80,983,000
Lines of communication cables	3,009,200 miles
Telephones	486,200
Wireless stations	445,500
Reception sets	34,227

Ammunition has not only grown in weight since the war began, but has become more complicated and difficult to make.

Wireless sets and other types of signal equipment have become much more elaborate.

A wide range of specialized stores, sometimes of a very bulky character, was made to facilitate the landings in Western Europe.

(e) Raw Materials

The output of iron ore in the United Kingdom has been increased by one-half since before the war, output in 1943 being 18,487,000 tons as compared with an average over the years 1935–8 of 12,417,000 tons.

The total steel production has been well above the pre-war average, being 13 million tons in 1943 as compared with an average of 11¼ million tons for the years 1935–8.

The production of timber has been increased, and in 1943 was more than four times as great as at the outbreak of war.

Some of the most outstanding increases in production have been made by the light metals industries to meet the requirements of aircraft and incendiary bomb production. Magnesium production is more than eleven times the pre-war rate (23,000 tons in 1943 as compared with an average of 2,000 tons in the years 1935–8). Production of aluminium rose from an average of 18,000 tons in 1935–8 to 56,000 tons in 1943.

11. THE ACHIEVEMENT OF BRITISH AGRICULTURE

'During the war immense advances have been made by the agricultural industry. The position of the farmers has been improved; the position of the labourers immeasurably improved.'

RT HON. WINSTON CHURCHILL, 21st March, 1943

Perspective

Because of the high degree of industrialization in Britain and the size of the population in relation to the total area, the country cannot be entirely self-supporting in foodstuffs. Nevertheless, British farmers have done a great war job in cutting down the import of food and relieving the strain on shipping to the utmost by bringing land back to cultivation and by improving the fertility and output of the land by the best possible methods of drainage and mechanized farming. The master plan in policy for production has been to change the island from a mainly grazing to a mainly arable country, to save a round voyage for a ship with every 10,000 tons of food grown.

The net loss of land to military and non-agricultural uses exceeded the area reclaimed or brought back to cultivation by 600,000 acres at the end of 1944. The increased production of British agriculture has, therefore, been achieved on an acreage smaller by that amount, by increasing the actual physical yield of the land and by increasing the proportion of crops available for direct human consumption.

Performance

As a result of the ploughing-up campaign, the area of arable land in the United Kingdom has increased by 43 per cent since shortly before the war. 7,000,000 acres of grassland have been ploughed up. Tillage has increased by 62 per cent.

In terms of shipping space saved, the United Kingdom's food production has increased by 120 per cent since before the war, and in terms of food values, by 70 per cent. The country is producing more food per acre than any country in the world, and also more food per man per acre.

Half the wheat used in the composition of national flour is home produced.

Production of wheat, barley and potatoes has more than doubled; production of oats and fruit is up by one-half and of sugar beet and vegetables by one-third.

To maintain the production of milk and to offset the reduction in imports of animal feeding-stuffs larger quantities of fodder crops have been grown.

To achieve a national output of nearly 7 million tons of ware potatoes the production of certified seed potatoes in the United Kingdom has been greatly increased from a figure of some 150,000 tons pre-war to over half a million tons in 1944.

There are nearly 1,708,300 allotments in the United Kingdom. In 1942 over £15,000,000 worth of vegetables was produced.

Britain now grows about half her sugar consumption, that is sufficient for the domestic sugar ration.

Farmers and County Committees in the United Kingdom have spent something like £100,000,000 during the war on machinery alone.

The United Kingdom is today the most highly mechanized farming country in Europe and has increased the numbers of tractors on the land by well over 170 per cent.

Under the Agricultural Goods and Services Scheme, assistance for farmers during the year 1942 was provided up to the value of almost £2 million sterling.

In order that land might receive appropriate treatment, the number of soil samples given laboratory tests by Advisory Chemists or tested in the field during 1943 cannot have been far short of 200,000.

Britain has closed the gap between the farmer and the scientist by setting up an Agricultural Improvement Council which ensures that modern research work is made known to farmers and applied in practice.

From September 1939 up to the end of August 1944, over 150,000 farm drainage schemes have been approved, affecting over 3¾ million acres and costing nearly £6,500,000.

In addition over £5,250,000 worth of schemes on minor water courses and £4,500,000 worth of main river schemes had been approved for execution during the war. Also, over £1,000,000 has been spent on drainage and machinery.

The result of the agricultural products programme has been that, coupled with the planning and control of food distribution, it had become possible by 1943 to maintain total food supplies at an adequate level, while at the same time reducing imports of food by 50 per cent, thus releasing an equivalent amount of shipping for other war purposes. The cost of this achievement was the sacrifice of 6½ million sheep, 2½ million pigs and 19¼ million poultry.

12. THE ACHIEVEMENT OF BRITISH INLAND TRANSPORT AND COMMUNICATIONS

'Throughout the period of the heavy German air-raids on this country the arteries of the nation, the railways, with their extensive dock undertakings, were subjected to intensive attacks... In spite of every enemy effort the traffic has been kept moving and the great flow of munitions proceeds. Results such as the railways have achieved are only won by blood and sweat.'

RT HON. WINSTON CHURCHILL, December 1943

Perspective

Wartime communications within Britain have been carried on under all the strain of threatened and actual air attack, of shortage of manpower, of change of emphasis and consequent reorganization. The General Post Office in particular has had not merely to maintain but greatly to increase its services for upon it has fallen the main burden of ensuring the facilities for rapid coordination within a country often the scene of active operations and always the base for others.

Britain's mainline railways cover 20,000 route miles. Central Wagon Control directs all wagons where they are most needed, and the Central Operating Conference confers every morning by telephone about big traffic movements. The intimate interrelation between railways and shipping in Britain's wartime transport was reflected by the merger of the Ministry of Shipping with the Ministry of Transport in 1941. Under the resultant Ministry of War Transport, shipping and inland transport have been rendered one continuous, coordinated operation from ships, through docks, railways, canals and roads.

Performance

British railways are carrying half as much traffic again as they did before the war. 113,000 railwaymen have been called up. 50 passenger trains have been lost in air raids.

1,623 million miles were run by trains operated by the mainline railways between the outbreak of war and the end of 1943.

More than 20,000 goods trains a week are being run, and nearly 1,000,000 loaded wagons. Through one mainline junction alone, 3,000 wagons pass every twenty-four hours in each direction.

4,052 million miles were run by loaded freight wagons in 1943. Since the beginning of the war the tonnage of freight carried by the railways and the average length of haul have both increased, so that the work done by the railways measured by net ton miles has risen by about 40 per cent.

Since the outbreak of war more than 353,000 special trains have been run for troops and their equipment.

The number of passenger-train miles is now 30 per cent below the pre-war level, and the average load carried by passenger trains is 125 per cent greater than before the war.

There are now no excursions at all. (In peacetime there were 17,500 half-day and evening excursions during the summer.) Instead there are 1,000 extra trains every day to carry workers to and from government factories alone.

In 1943 locomotives spent 7,500,000 more hours in traffic than in 1938, while the number available for work had increased by only 1 per cent.

Over 35,000 railway-owned wagons are repaired each week.

Amenities of travel have gone. In peacetime there were 870 restaurant car services in operation. Now there are none.

At the time of Dunkirk, 620 emergency trains were run in eight days, carrying 300,000 troops from seven ports in the south-east of England. At the busiest time, 110 special trains were worked in twenty-four hours.

At the end of 1941, locomotives and other rolling-stock were rushed to Persia to speed up supplies to Russia over the Trans-Persian Railway. 143 locomotives, specially equipped, with tenders and spare parts, were sent, and 1,600 steel-frame 12-ton wagons were built in record time. By working night and day the assembling works fitted together the 1,800 parts of each wagon so that one was completed every thirty-seven minutes.

Preparations for the North African Expedition involved the running of 440 special troop trains, 680 special freight trains, and 15,000 railway wagons by ordinary goods services, to carry men and materials to the embarkation ports.

From 26th March, 1944, to the completion of the initial D-Day moves, British railways ran 24,459 special troop, ammunition and stores trains. Among other vital war traffics these trains carried some 7,000 vehicles including tanks. More than 6,000 wagon-loads of supplies and equipment were also sent by ordinary goods trains. During the three weeks before D-Day, the movement of special trains reached its peak. In one week all wartime records were surpassed with the running of 3,636 special trains, and the total for the three weeks was no fewer than 9,679 trains.

Road transport, by reason of its flexibility, has been of great service in the war effort both on the passenger and goods sides, and has been especially valuable in meeting emergency calls.

Considerable restrictions have been imposed on bus services. In 1941 long-distance express services were drastically curtailed, with the result that the total mileage of all bus routes in the country was reduced by 40 per cent. Many bus undertakings have had to carry from 30 to 50 per cent more passengers than in 1938.

Long-distance road goods vehicles have been taken over by the Government and are operated by the Ministry of War Transport. This direct form of control is intended to concentrate the traffic in the fewest possible vehicles and to ensure that enough vehicles are available in areas where they are urgently needed.

During the winter of 1943–4, this organization performed invaluable work in helping to move the immense cargoes which were being unloaded in the ports, in transporting meat to army camps and depots, in carrying prefabricated parts of ships for assembly at the shipyards, and in moving other loads too unwieldy to go by rail.

The organization was also assigned an important part in the preparations for the landings in France. Its job included the movement to embarkation ports of large numbers of landing craft, some of them weighing as much as 40 tons, together with cased gliders, aero-engines, steam-rollers and bulldozers, and thousands of tons of foodstuffs. During the peak period the organization was moving cargo at the rate of over 1,000,000 tons a week.

Canals, too, have been brought under governmental control. 10,000 boats and barges carrying 1,000,000 tons a month help to reduce pressure on the railways. Half of this total is represented by fuel, the remainder is made up of heavy bulk cargoes such as building materials, munitions, fertilisers, manufactured foodstuffs and home-grown grain.

The canals' part in the preparations for D-Day consisted in carrying blocks of traffic which would normally have gone by road or rail, thus releasing vehicles for more urgent work.

Coastal shipping is being used to the fullest possible extent both for offloading from deep-sea vessels and also for long-distance carriage of coal and other home products. There has been a marked increase in the tonnage carried by each ship.

Coasters have also played an indispensable part in military operations in the Mediterranean and in carrying troops and supplies to France.

The General Post Office plays an important part in the communications of Britain. It operates 24,000 post offices, 5,800 telephone exchanges, 51,400 telephone call offices and 3,700,000 telephone stations.

Since the outbreak of war the Post Office has not only had to provide for an increase in almost every branch of its normal business, but for an ever-increasing range of new activities under constantly changing conditions, including measures for the continuance of services during and after air raids.

Teleprinter working has been adopted on all but the lightly loaded telegraph routes. In 1942–3 the number of inland telegrams handled was 64,000,000, compared with about 48,000,000 a year before the war.

The Post Office is responsible for the maintenance of communications with the police, ambulance and other similar services. The warning of the approach of enemy air-craft is spread by the ordinary Post Office network to points from which the air raid siren warnings are operated.

Britain has built an elaborate interconnected oil pipeline system extending over 1,000 miles from North-West ports to the Channel. Five million gallons flow through it daily. Later the pipelines were carried under the Channel to serve the advancing 21st Army Group.

The system is studded with scores of secret underground storage tanks for holding large reserve stocks. This line places fuel supplies directly into the centre of nests of airfields, and eases the strain on other methods of transport.

13. THE ACHIEVEMENT OF BRITISH WAR ECONOMY

'This is no time for ease and comfort. It is the time to dare and endure. That is why we are rationing ourselves, even while our resources are expanding. That is why we mean to regulate every ton that is carried across the sea and make sure that it is carried solely for the purpose of victory.'

RT HON. WINSTON CHURCHILL, 27th January, 1940

Perspective

Britain has mobilized her resources for war in four main ways: by increasing the total volume of production; by reducing civilian consumption; by drawing on capital at home; by drawing on capital abroad. The national resources have been switched over from a peacetime economy to a war economy by direct control and rationing and by financial methods. Direct control applies to labour, raw materials and industrial capacity, to imports and exports, to the amount and type of goods manufactured and supplied. Civilian consumption has been notably reduced not only in quantity but also in quality, and that very extensively.

Performance

(a) Taxation

In 1944, it is estimated, about 36 per cent of Britain's gross national income went in taxes, including compulsory contributions for social insurance and war risks or damage. This compares with 22 per cent in 1938.

In the financial year 1944–5, the British Inland Revenue netted in taxes nearly four times the amount collected in 1938–9: £2,029 million as against £520 million. And that relates only to the budget of the central government. (Inland Revenue includes Income Tax, Surtax, Estate Duties, Stamps (Inland Revenue), National Defence Contribution, Excess Profits Tax, etc.)

53 per cent of total Government expenditure in 1944–5 was provided by taxation and other Government revenue.

The number of income tax payers increased from 4 million in 1938–9 to 13 million in 1943–4.

In Britain a single person earning £500 a year now pays £156 of it away in income tax; if he earns £1,000 he pays £381. On unearned income the tax is even higher. A married couple with two children and an unearned income of £100,000 would have £5,830 left after taxation – 94 per cent of their income gone.

Indirect taxation in 1944–5 brought in £1,105 million, against £376 million in 1938–9.

Twenty cigarettes now cost 2s. 4d. in Britain; three-quarters of the price (1s. 9d.) goes to the Exchequer in duty.

The duty on beer, at the present reduced average strength, accounts for well over half the price (7½d. out of 1s. a pint).

Even on tea, the staple drink of British working families, 6d. is paid in duty on a pound, bringing the cost to 2s. 10d.

On a wide range of luxury goods a purchase tax amounting to 100 per cent of the wholesale value must be paid. And on a very wide range of other goods for civilian consumption there is a purchase tax of one-third or one-sixth of the wholesale value.

(b) Restriction

The adult people of Britain are on small rations of meat, milk, eggs, butter, margarine, cooking fats, bacon, ham, sugar, tea, preserves, sweets and chocolate.

Purchase-control by a flexible rationing system by 'points' further applies to canned meat, canned fish, canned beans, dried fruit, rice, sago, tapioca, dried pulses, canned fruit, canned peas, canned tomatoes, canned milk, breakfast cereals, oat flakes, syrup, treacle and biscuits.

There is now no white bread in Britain, no bananas, and little imported fruit at all.

27 per cent less fresh meat, 56 per cent fewer shell eggs, 35 per cent less sugar, 69 per cent less butter, and 56 per cent less fresh fruit are being eaten on an average in Britain now than before the war. Potato consumption has gone up 54 per cent.

Standardization of many commodities, and 'zoning' of their distribution so that cross-hauls are cut out, saves internal transport. Shipping space is saved by using milk and eggs in their dehydrated form. Dried egg enables the equivalent of shell eggs to be imported in a fifth of the tonnage.

The ordinary person who cannot show urgent necessity for using his car is allowed no petrol at all.

Travel by rail is considerably more expensive and more restricted than in normal times. There are no more excursions or special holiday trains in Britain.

The production of many articles such as motor cars, refrigerators, pianos, vacuum cleaners and lawnmowers has been completely suspended from 1942 or earlier, while the production of cutlery, wireless sets and valves, bicycles, watches and fountain pens has been drastically curtailed. For example, only 540,000 civilian bicycles were produced in 1943 as compared with 1,600,000 in 1935, and the production of civilian wireless sets during the same period was reduced from 1,900,000 to 50,000.

British potteries normally produced sixty-seven shapes of cup. Now they are producing three. The normal range of hardware products has been cut by 60 per cent.

Clothes are strictly rationed and the supply available is about half what it was before the war.

Only standardized 'utility' furniture may now be made. This economical furniture conforms to specified descriptions and measurements, and there is only enough of it to supply urgent needs, such as those of the newly married or bombed-out. Purchase is by permit.

Linen sheets are no longer made. The manufacture of quilts and bedspreads has been cut to a minimum and no tablecloths at all are produced.

Purchases of furniture, furnishings and household textiles have been reduced to about one-fifth of the peace-time quantity, and to one-third in the case of hardware.

Concentration of production had been applied by March 1944 to nearly seventy branches of industry. 3,620 establishments had been closed, thus freeing manpower and plant for essential war purposes.

(c) Saving

During five years of war Britain's housewives and local authorities collected nearly 6 million tons of salvage.

Over 5,000,000 tons was the total of scrap metal collected from all sources from November 1939 to May 1944.

Over 100 million books have so far been collected in a national drive to collect books for the armed forces, for restocking bombed libraries and for salvage.

During the winter of 1942–3 British domestic and industrial consumers of coal effected an economy of

11,000,000 tons in response to the request and advice of the Government. This saving was 3,000,000 tons greater than the advance official estimate.

There were over 298,000 Savings Groups in the United Kingdom in December 1944.

Over £469 million was raised for the war savings campaign in War Weapons Weeks held between September 1940 and June 1941. This is an approximate average of £10 per head of the British population.

Over £545½ million was raised during Warships Weeks between October 1941 and March 1942. The amount raised in England and Wales alone (nearly £478 million) was equivalent to the cost of building 5 battleships, 4 aircraft carriers, 45 cruisers, 300 destroyers, 160 corvettes, 33 submarines, 267 minesweepers, 124 motor torpedo-boats, 117 depot ships, sloops, monitors, etc.

Over £616 million was raised for the war savings campaign during Wings for Victory Weeks between March 1943 and July 1943.

Over £626 million was raised during the Salute the Soldier campaign between March 1944 and July 1944.

Over £8,467 million had been lent to the Government up to December 1944. That is an average of £177 per head of the British population.

Out of every £100 received by the average British citizen in 1943 he saved £19 – and paid in taxes £36 – leaving only £45 for 'living'.

14. THE ACHIEVEMENT OF THE BRITISH SPIRIT

The British spirit has been a factor in the Allied war potential of greater importance than any strategic effort or industrial output. Hard as it may be to measure, it must be included in a summary of the British achievement.

A dogged perseverance has been part of it. The very unwillingness to be diverted from everyday pursuits, which brought the British people to so late a realization of their peril and the world's, engendered a deep determination to see the war through, at whatever cost, to the only possible conclusion. So Britain became the point round which all resistance to aggression could coalesce.

Endurance has certainly been called for and has not been lacking. 'Grim and gay' aptly described the way the British felt and acted under the Blitz and the threat of invasion.

Exaltation has had its moments too. It was the key to the British mood in 1940, when the sense of danger and responsibility gave to the national character a sharper identity than ever before.

A determination to plan for a future beyond victory has helped to sustain the British spirit throughout the war and has produced the spectacle of a nation with its life in peril nevertheless carrying through domestic reforms of unparalleled magnitude.

This spirit has certainly had effects beyond the bounds of the nation. The planning and organization of the Grand Alliance have been the fruit of a popular determination to make friends of Allies, expressed and interpreted by wise leadership.

The grand achievement of the British spirit has been that it has risen to the occasion in many hours full of peril, bringing salvation to Britain, to her Allies and to the world.